MINISTRY TO THE HOSPITALIZED

Ministry
to the
Hospitalized

by
Gerald R. Niklas
and
Charlotte Stefanics

PAULIST PRESS
New York/Paramus/Toronto

Library of Congress
Catalog Card Number: 75-22986

ISBN: 0-8091-1899-8

Published by Paulist Press
Editorial Office: 1865 Broadway, N.Y., N.Y. 10023
Business Office: 400 Sette Drive, Paramus, N.J. 07652

Printed and bound in the
United States of America

Contents

Preface

Three community hospitals initiated volunteer chaplaincy programs in and near Springfield, Ohio in recent years. Local clergymen volunteered to serve as chaplains for one week at these hospitals. In order that they might be effective in their ministry to the sick, orientation programs were set up in each of the hospitals consisting of 20-25 hours of lectures and discussions on topics that the volunteer chaplains thought would be helpful in their work. However, the clergy could find little reference material to complement these seminars. Less than one-third of the hospitals in the United States have salaried chaplaincy services, and since the AMA has strongly supported chaplaincy services, many small community hospitals elsewhere will initiate them and need a book to complement their orientation programs.

Other clergy who cannot participate in such programs are eager to improve their ministry to the sick and will benefit from a book giving them insights into the emotions of sick people with their various illnesses as well as some simple counseling techniques that will aid in this work.

Seminarians too are interested in acquiring skills in this area. Many of them are totally unacquainted with the emotions of sick people and know little of the modern hospital. A number of women religious have recently become engaged in pastoral work and are now seeking more knowledge about hospital visitation and ministry to the shut-ins of the parish, as well as at times serving as chaplains to some of the nursing homes within the parish limits. As a result, there is a growing need for them to receive assistance in their new apostolate. Finally, nurses and other workers in the health field are anxious to broaden their understanding of the sick person.

1

We hope that the insights gleaned from the pages of this book will enable pastoral counselors to effectively bring Christ to the sick and their relatives. Further, we trust that it will make a contribution to the field of pastoral care by combining the knowledge and experience of a hospital chaplain and a nurse clinical specialist in psychiatric mental health.

However, it should be realized that no book in itself will enable a member of the helping profession to come to grips with his own feelings about sickness and death. Only the individual person with the assistance of a leader can accomplish this task which is necessary for a person to effectively minister to the sick.

We are deeply indebted to our three typists, Mrs. Glenda Rogers, Mrs. Joyce Thomas, and Miss Mary Jean Niklas who have typed and retyped these chapters until they reached their final form. We also express our gratitude to Sister Mary LaSalette, R.S.M., and Mrs. Natalie Margolis who have read our manuscripts with a critical eye and offered many helpful suggestions in improving our work. Finally, we thank the editors of *Homiletic and Pastoral Review* for granting permission to print Chapters Two and Eight, both of which appeared in their magazine before revision for insertion in this book.

1. Ministering to the Common Emotional Needs of the Hospitalized Patient

To have a better understanding of the patient's response to hospitalization one needs to have some knowledge of the hospital world and what happens to the person who enters that world.

The modern hospital is a highly complex bureaucratic system that functions under managerial methods. It can be simply explained that it is like a city within a city, functioning very similarly. The hospital organization has a line of authority, division of labor, rules, regulations and policies that are necessary for the greatest efficiency to deliver health services to the community in which it exists. In the hospital community the first line of authority is composed of select members of the larger community who serve on a governing board. Their function is to determine if the hospital is meeting the health needs of the community and if efficiency is maintained within the organization. The hierarchy continues down the line from the governing board to the administrator, the directors, then to the supervisors, and funneling down, so that each department has a head to whom all subordinates are responsible. Each department is autonomous but is part of the greater whole, maintaining adequate functions to give quality health services.

This social organization is also "big business," and the personnel within this system become much the same as in other large businesses. They tend to get lost in the lines of authority and the divisions of labor and feel insignificant in their roles in serving the patient.

The department heads expect their personnel to function according to a particular set of rules, regulations and policies.

Defined roles are developed for each category of personnel who tend to become so intent on efficiency toward supposedly smoother operations that the patient's needs are sometimes assumed to be met when in actuality the patient feels alienated. He can easily feel lost as patient care becomes routine, automated and subject to various departments who are carrying out the functions to diagnose or treat his illness. He is awakened at a certain hour because tasks must be performed by or at a certain time. In fact, his entire day is more or less regimented according to a schedule that supposedly facilitates hospital efficiency. Very often he does not fully understand the purpose of the procedures or tests since no one explains them clearly to him. This causes the patient to become apprehensive, especially when he is experiencing a major illness. Patients will tell you often how they are ignored or how no one seems to be available to explain to them what is actually going on. The patient entering this bureaucratic system is processed in much the same fashion as in any other bureaucracy, thereby contributing to the dehumanization process. Thus hospitals which exist for community members seeking health care have become so enmeshed in bureaucracy with its lines of authority and forms that they find it very difficult to keep their focus of attention centered on the patient who is the only reason for their existence.

The nursing personnel, who try to coordinate the care services for patients and give them quality care, are gravely inhibited. Nurses are educated to assess their patients' needs and to intervene effectively so that they can meet those needs through individualized care. Rarely is the nurse able to have charge of patient care because of the many rules that govern her services. Ideally, the nurse should have charge of the care of the patient just as the medical staff has charge over the cure of the patient. Both disciplines are necessary and they should complement each other in the best interests of the patient. This rarely happens because in many hospitals nurses still do not have full control of nursing services. The nurse is caught in the system between two lines of authority—the medical staff which in many instances still views the nurse as subordinate to the physician, and the administration which demands that the nurse function according to the rules or policies it decides is best for the patient, without ever consulting the nurse. In their frustration nurses complain about the system where they cannot give quality care and the patients' needs are not adequately met.

Each hospital organization has its own philosophy concerning its purpose in the delivery of health services. The philosophy includes beliefs and values which the hospital personnel assimilate, creating a specific culture within the hospital. Often the personnel assume that patients understand them when in reality they do not. Personnel often forget that their values, beliefs, attitudes, ways of doing things, and understanding of the situation may be completely different from those of their patients.[1]

The Admission Process

In most hospitals the admission process does an excellent job of making a person feel like a statistic and anomie. Most hospitals have a definite time for admissions, so from the very beginning the patient must submit to the routine of the hospital system. A person who plans his admission will experience less anxiety than the person who is admitted as an emergency case. Therefore the person who plans ahead may have made preparations to have certain major responsibilities taken care of at home or at work so that he can concentrate more on his need to get well.

During the initial admission the patient is seen first by a clerk, a total stranger, who asks him personal, possibly embarrassing questions about his financial status and how the bill will be paid. He is then assigned a hospital number in a particular unit where he is given a bed in a room not of his choosing. If he has a roommate, he too is a total stranger. At a time when he needs a familiar person and security he is among strangers.

After passing the hospital admissions clerk, he is sent to the unit to which he is assigned. A nurse or one of the nursing personnel greets him, sometimes very casually, or he is called by name from his admission sheet to verify his identity. An ident-band is placed around his wrist. He is taken back to his room, shown his bed and where he can put his belongings. More often than not, he is asked to undress, put on a hospital gown and get into bed because it is procedure. He is then subjected to another series of questions, such as his reason for coming to the hospital, his medical history and a personal inquiry by the nursing personnel for their record. His temperature and blood pressure are usually taken; then he is given a small bottle and asked to give a specimen of urine as soon as possible, because all admission specimens must be in the lab at a certain time. He is given a quick briefing on hospital routine and how to call the nurse if he needs anything; then he is told that the resident doctor will be in later to examine him.

During this ordeal, his anxiety increases because as much as he would like to ask questions, he doesn't. Somehow he feels very dependent and inadequate, and remains quiet, trying to cooperate. If the patient's wife accompanied him, he tries to suppress his anxiety to lessen her concern. As a result both are apprehensive.

Often you hear nursing personnel refer to a patient as "the cholecystectomy in Room 214, Bed B," which indicates non-involvement. The entire atmosphere makes him feel as if he must fit into the role of "the expected behavior of a patient," whatever that means. Travelbee states that the "patient" is an abstraction, a set of expectations personified by tasks to be performed, treatments to carry out, an illness, or a room number.[2]

This threatens the person's self-concept, for his self identity is lost among the many other cases, and even though he knows that he isn't the only one, he feels he wants to be recognized as a person, as a someone. How great a patient feels when he is approached and called by his name: someone knows him as a person, is aware of him as an individual.

When the relatives of the sick person leave for home, he is left alone with his thoughts. Often the patient worries about how long he will have to remain in the hospital and whether his job will be there when he gets back. He also worries about his family and how will they function without him. If the patient is a mother of a family, she has this same concern. If she has small children, she worries if they will be cared for properly, and how her husband will do his work efficiently if he's worried about her.

The sick person has left the familiar environment of his family unit, where he felt secure, loved and valued, and where he is his own person making decisions independently as well as interdependently. The hospital environment deprives the person of much of his independence and the privilege of the concern of his family, as seen by the restriction of visitation of family members during his illness. This is evident by the visiting hours the hospital has established and the difficulty the family experiences in obtaining permission to remain with the critically ill person after visiting hours. The patient's wishes are not taken into consideration, since the routine is established for maintaining efficiency in carrying out the functions of the hospital organization. Efforts are being made to study the hospital organization in order to give better health care, but we have a long way to go before the bureaucracy can be flexible enough to make the patient the top priority.

Since hospital personnel rarely take the time to view a patient as an individual and since procedures, diagnostic tests and various treatments are explained to him in hospital jargon or medical terms that sound like a foreign language, is it any wonder that he feels like an alien? Another result of the many tests, in addition to the checks on temperature, blood pressure, etc., is that the hospital is rarely a place for a person to rest. Sometimes, though, a person actually enjoys the many interruptions of hospitalization in order to meet his high dependency needs. Such a person will fake an illness to seek the protectiveness of the hospital because he cannot function independently in society. However this is not too common and is in itself an illness.

Quite naturally then, the person entering the hospital environment is experiencing many emotions, whether his illness is acute, chronic, or terminal. His entire being is affected as he is confronted with his aloneness that reminds him of his mortality, increasing his fear and anxiety levels. He becomes concerned with himself and his world closes in on him. The things that used to interest him suddenly lose their hold. His favorite TV programs no longer are appealing as he now focuses all his attention on himself and his sickness. In addition, he expects those around him to see him as he sees himself, presuming they understand how he feels. Of the many feelings the hospitalized person is experiencing, the greatest one is fear. He fears what the doctor might find, what the tests will indicate, and in general what the future holds for him.[3]

A Patient's Reaction to His Illness

How a sick person reacts to his illness depends upon his view of it. He may take it as a matter of course and go along with everything, knowing that it will only be a short while, or he may be annoyed, considering the sickness a disruption in his busy life, especially if it is not too serious. This is often seen in the case of an executive who feels that his business cannot function without him. Frequently this is true, so he carries on business from his hospital bed. If his illness is terminal or debilitating, he may be experiencing denial, so his behavior is one that resembles a person who is enjoying a relative state of well-being. Underneath he feels: "It can't be me. I'm sure the diagnosis is incorrect." He vacillates between a positive and a negative attitude, depending upon his view of his illness.

Some individuals regard illness and suffering as an intrusion God has sent into their lives to punish them for some past faults or failures. As a result they feel guilty and become agitated and uncomfortable. Others view their illness with confusion, not knowing what to make of it. They feel very much alone, and this loneliness increases as the hospital personnel communicate with him by using small talk. Rarely if ever does anyone help him to verbalize his confusion and anxieties. Procedures are often not explained; he asks why certain blood tests are done, only to receive the response, "It's routine," or he asks about certain procedures only to be told that he should discuss that with his doctor. Doctors are great in helping to keep everything a mystery by not sharing valuable information with patients because they know what is best for the patient. As a result, the sick person may become angry and very disillusioned with his physician. A patient has the right to know and needs to feel that he has something to say concerning his illness.

There are still others who regard their illness chiefly as a great threat to their life or their self-image, and consequently they become fearful and very anxious. In an attempt to cope with these emotions, a person may react with hostility and resentment to recapture an appearance and a feeling of strength. He asserts himself by being demanding or stubborn in an effort to regain his equilibrium. A patient angrily snaps "What do I have to do to get anything around here?" or "I asked for pain medication over an hour ago and no one has brought me a thing." On the other hand, the sick person may react by retreating from others, attempting to find relief in avoidance and withdrawal. Often such a person feels that no one really understands his needs, so he isolates himself by refusing to socialize with the other patients.

Finally, in an attempt to cope with his intense feelings, he may learn to play "the game" in order to survive the ordeal of hospitalization, and so he becomes known as a "good patient." Being a "good patient," he tries to maintain a certain pleasing behavior. By keeping his feelings under control, he hopes to be accepted and liked by the staff who in turn will give him good nursing care. Such a person feels compelled to submit to the medical regime because this is what is expected of a "good patient," yet he resents the dependent role he assumes. Thus he becomes angry and hostile but cannot express these feelings because according to his standards of conduct an adult must be in control of himself at all times and also must be considerate of the way his behavior affects others.

In an effort to predict how the sick person will react to his illness and hospitalization, Lisa Robinson explains: "The individual contemplating admission to a hospital will cope with the stress of his hospitalization in the same manner that he would cope with other major stresses in his life."[4] His ability to meet the stress of hospitalization also depends a great deal on how he views hospitalization either from previous admissions which may have been pleasant or unpleasant experiences, or if it is his first experience, or he can have many thoughts and feelings about the hospital and the personnel from hearsay. Friends may say to the patient, "When you go in that place be prepared for the worst. The last time I was in that place they almost took me to surgery instead of my roommate." "You really gotta be careful with your things; I had some money stolen there." "I had a friend who went to surgery for a simple appendectomy and his heart stopped when they put him to sleep; he almost didn't make it."

Each person then responds uniquely depending upon his coping mechanisms, his preconceived ideas about the hospital, and his ability to adapt to a new life situation. A pastoral visitor views his people as individuals, observes non-verbal communication and listens with an openness to hear how the hospitalization has affected them. He views the transformation of the individual to becoming a patient: the wellness to the illness phenomena.

If the sick person copes with his fear by expressing anger and hostility, the nursing personnel label him as the eccentric, demanding or problem patient. This depersonalization is the result of our highly technocratic society that often seems to view others as categories instead of individuals. Hospital personnel are part of that technocracy and the complex bureaucratic system that places them into categories with expected behavior to perform a particular job with expertise.

Role of the Clergy

The role of the clergyman is then of great value, not only as a religious person but as a person who is truly concerned about the patient as an individual. Coming to know how the hospitalized person is responding to his environment and illness he develops the art of listening as well as the capacity to observe non-verbal behavior. Patients may open up very easily when approached with the friendly casual greeting, "How are you doing?"

Anyone involved in helping those who are ill and suffering

must have some concept of man; otherwise, he sees him only from a personal unique frame of reference. If you view man as having value, dignity and a free choice, you can establish a relationship with another human being and help him evaluate his life situation in such a way that he becomes responsible for his own choices. This is most important when the patient blames others for his misfortunes, becoming very angry and hostile, or when he is unable to find any meaning in his life.

To be effective as a minister, one needs to have an awareness of oneself as a person. Values, attitudes and beliefs about life are very important. All too often biases are transmitted through non-verbal behavior and may block the ability to understand how the patient is trying to cope. This happens when the pastoral visitor thinks he is hearing the patient when in reality he is hearing from his own frame of reference. The patient knows when he is not being heard. If the patient says to you, "You don't seem to understand," or "I need to clarify what I just said," he is telling you he does not feel you have moved into his frame of reference and he is not being heard.

A function of the pastoral visitor is to help the sick person consider his life situation realistically so that he can grow from the experience. This is done by first establishing a relatedness with the patient, using a deliberate approach to learn how he feels and views his life situation. This involves being able to communicate effectively without preventing the individual from expressing himself. For communication to be open, a nonjudgmental accepting atmosphere needs to be developed in order for the patient to feel that someone is genuinely interested and concerned about him as a person. This is done when non-verbally you observe or assess the anxiety level of a person and try to lessen it, by focusing on the person, retaining a calm relaxed manner. Listen intently to what he is saying. Respond in such a way that he can continue to express his thoughts and feelings freely. Reflecting on the person's feelings or thoughts helps him to gain insight into himself and how he is struggling to cope with his situation realistically.

Your non-verbal behavior speaks loud and clear to the patient the same as his non-verbal behavior tells you how he is feeling. Body movements and gestures are means of expression which when observed need to be interpreted as they offer a valuable help to a deeper understanding of the patient's communication. Having adequate knowledge of non-verbal behavior will enhance the minister's ability to understand more fully what transpires during the interaction—his facial expressions of sadness, worry, or if he moves continuously about as he tries to explain his feelings. If he is sitting in a chair, is he on the edge of it as if he is ready to get up and go somewhere, or if he is in bed is he picking at the bed clothes, does he clasp and unclasp his hands? Knowledge of body language is of utmost importance, for he may be saying one thing and non-verbally telling you something else.

Listening is a very important part of communication since it requires being actively involved with the person in his situation. Trying to hear him from his frame of reference is difficult since it requires knowledge and discipline of oneself. This ability to transcend into the world of the other, to experience his feelings with him, gives you a deeper understanding of how the patient is experiencing his illness and suffering. The only way you can know another person is if he opens his world and invites you in to share himself with you. One way a person opens his world is by expressing his thoughts, his feelings, and makes it possible to observe how he behaves. Being in the situation, sharing and experiencing with the person, you come to know how he views himself in the world in which he now participates. He may be sharing his fears and apprehensions with you: your role is to help him to understand his feelings so he can cope more realistically with his life situation and grow from the experience. In a therapeutic relationship Van Kaam says, that the person should grow to the insight that his life situation is not a power which determines him totally into the deepest core of his being, but he should realize that he cannot escape his life, that he may give form to it, he may shape it or recreate it.[5] Listening is a very important part of the interaction between the pastoral visitor and the person who needs help as he copes with his hospitalization. It is a skill that must be developed.

It takes time to break through the barrier before he will

open to you, but by maintaining an accepting attitude he will gradually feel you are sincere and then he'll begin to tell you his concerns. Your accepting attitude is conveyed by the relaxed position you assume when listening, maintaining a comfortable closeness, nodding your head in agreement or understanding. You can respond by "I understand what you are saying," "I appreciate how you feel," "You must be experiencing a great deal of suffering" and possibly using touch that says to the other person I'm with you or I comfort you. Touch often transmits to the other person when words are not necessary, but you must know when and how to use it therapeutically.

Listening for his fears, reflecting his feelings and offering alternate views may help him to develop a realistic perception of his situation and enable him to cope with it adequately. Arriving at a realistic perception is done by evaluating earlier coping mechanisms that are no longer adequate and helping the person to view his situation from a different perspective. This can be done by encouraging him to communicate his fears if he has never talked about them with anyone. However, a person may feel—why talk about it, no one can help me, while another may think that it is a sign of weakness to admit he is afraid and anxious about his illness. Using gentle persuasion, a good samaritan assists such a person verbalize his fears and after listening empathetically, he reflects them back to the ill person making him realize he is understood and accepted with his fears. This gives him insight into himself and moves him toward greater awareness of his life situation. Since he has experienced support and received assistance in working through his feelings, he can more readily and realistically cope with his illness. Just knowing that he is understood, without being judged, is itself a tremendous source of strength that will enable the sick person to grow from his experience. On the other hand, using cliches, such as, "Don't worry, God will take care of everything," has little or no value especially when the patient is angry with God, asking, "How can God be so cruel to me? I've suffered so much all my life." Telling the ill person he will be all right blocks communications since he may know he will not.

The patient, experiencing fear, anxiety and loneliness, becomes concerned with himself. He may try to conceal his feelings about his hospitalization but if you observe clues of anxiety you can explore those feelings with him. He may tell you he is fine and appear very tense, irritable, and fidgety. He may look as if he is very uncomfortable and you begin to feel his tenseness. Using a deliberate approach by asking him, "How are things going?" or "How is everything with you today?"; a good samaritan can be alert for clues, especially of denial, annoyance or real concern. The person in denial speaks in a way that conveys he is really accepting everything, or he's trying to play the role of the "good patient." He says he's doing fine and has nothing to worry about because his doctor knows best or God will take care of everything. A religious person responds by asking, "Does it make you feel safe that God will take care of everything for you?" This can be an opening question that the visitor uses to pursue the ill person's concept of God and his relationship to God.

The Patient's Concept of God and His Attitude toward Suffering

Some patients have a very difficult time coping with their illness because of their concept of God. A patient may view God as a very strict, demanding punitive Father because his own father was this way. Every time he did anything wrong, his father immediately punished him severely to show his displeasure at such conduct. Naturally, when such people are taught about God the Father in heaven, they presume he is similar to his father on earth. If this same father showed little or no expression of love to his child, he will then have this one-sided view of God which only considers his justice and has no insight into his merciful, loving and forgiving nature. In his childhood such a person probably was taught the story of the punishment of Adam and Eve, of the great flood at the time of Lot punishing the people for their sins and the destruction of the cities of Sodom and Gomorrah to atone for their unnatural vices. In his education the story of the patience of God with Moses and the Jewish people in the desert was not taught, nor his forgiveness as illustrated in the accounts of the prodigal son and the woman caught in adultery. As a result, this person's concept of God is warped and causes him to feel very guilty, viewing illness and suffering as a punishment from God. Such a sick person often asks, "Why me at this time?" "God can't be love if I have to suffer such terrible agony," or "God must be punishing me for my past sins."

A woman hospitalized for ulcers read the book of Revelation, always emphasizing those passages concerning final judgment and punishment. Even when she read verses urging her to have hope, she glossed over them and kept in the front of her mind sin and God's justice. She viewed God as "I got you in your sins" type of person who enjoys seeing people suffer and going to hell. During the first call on this patient, she told the visitor she was suffering for her sins. When he asked her to name one serious sin she was suffering for, she responded, "I don't know any offhand, but we're committing sins all day that we don't know about."

With such a patient the pastoral visitor tries to convey a balanced concept of God by sharing something of his own image of God. He recalls incidents from Sacred Scripture which exemplify the mercy, forgiveness, and love of God. The pastoral person, sharing those passages which are most meaningful to him, might mention the acceptance Christ offered Peter after his denial, the tender love which Christ displayed to Judas even after he predicted his betrayal, or the merciful words of Christ hanging on the cross, "Father, forgive them, for they know not what they do." It cannot be expected that the sick person will change his concept of God immediately, but hopefully this sharing will cause him to reconsider his idea of God, incorporating some aspects of mercy and love into it.

In connection with the sick person's concept of God it is important also to discuss his attitude toward suffering. Normally, a patient freely verbalizes his feelings and thoughts when he knows a good samaritan is concerned about him. So by listening carefully the spiritual leader learns how the patient views suffering, learns his attitudes toward suffering. As was said, some view all suffering as punishment for their sins, others as something evil to avoid at all costs and in which there is absolutely no meaning, others look upon suffering as something God permits to bring about a greater good, others regard suffering as something that is part of life, a cross a person simply must accept, while others view suffering as something nobody likes, but that it is a part of life and that some meaning can be discovered in all suffering. Theodore Bovet comments on this point, "Normally nobody likes to suffer. We all attempt insofar as this is possible, to prevent or curtail suffering. When we cannot prevent, suppress or diminish our suffering because we lack control over our internal or external environment we have no other recourse but to change our attitude towards suffering."[6]

When a spiritual leader offers alternate views about suffering, he opens other possibilities for the patient. The pastoral visitor doesn't force any particular view on the sick person, but does mention other attitudes toward suffering so that he has the freedom of choosing between several possibilities. It is beneficial if the clergyman shares his own attitude with the patient as one option for him to choose.

A good samaritan has a great opportunity to help patients so they do not view suffering as something totally negative, so they may find some meaning in it. In his book *Man's Search For Meaning*, Victor Frankl says, "Whenever one is confronted with an inescapable, unavoidable situation, whenever one has to face a fate which cannot be changed; e.g., an incurable disease, such as inoperable cancer; just then one is given a last chance to actualize the highest value, to fulfill the deepest meaning, the meaning in suffering. For what matters above all is the attitude we take toward suffering, the attitude in which we take our sufferings upon ourselves."[7]

The clergy urge the sick person to discover some meaning in his illness, but it is not his responsibility to find the meaning. Rather the responsibility rests on the shoulders of the sick and the clergy works with him to find some meaning. In other words, the spiritual leader hunts with the patient for a "why" so that he can bear up with the "how." Victor Frankl gives an example of a fellow prisoner in the Nazi prison camp who found meaning in suffering and dying. This man made a pact with God that his suffering and death would save his spouse from a painful death. He did not die for nothing as a result; he died for a cause, his wife.[8]

In order to be effective, the minister first clarifies his own theology on suffering; he reconciles for himself an all loving God with tragedy. If he has not done his "homework," he only hinders the patient as he gropes to find meaning. If the person is religious, the clergyman uses the Bible to assist him. Personally, I find comfort in Paul's letter to the Romans (11:33), "Oh the depth of the riches of the wisdom and of the knowledge of God. How incomprehensible are his judgments and how unsearchable his ways." For this passage makes me realize I'll never find a completely satisfactory answer. That suffering as a mystery is further illustrated by the account of the man born blind who was brought to our Lord with the question, "Who has sinned, this man or his parents that he should be born blind?" Our Lord never answered that question, but added this comforting thought about suffering—it is not punishment for sin. "Neither has this man sinned, nor his parents . . ." (John 9:2, 3). Some peace comes to my questioning mind when I am reminded of the fact that a servant is not above his master. Since my master Christ suffered, then suffering has to be part of my life too. Again, it must be noted that my personal attitude is never forced upon a patient, but only stirs up his thinking so that he can find his own meaning.

In conclusion, the clergy involved in assisting the ill person through his hospital experience needs to have an understanding of the hospital bureaucratic system. The hospital organization exists to deliver health care services to the community it serves, and the person processed into the system as a patient experiences fears, anxieties and alienation. The pastoral visitor who has an awareness of himself as a person, with knowledge of the human condition, can be most beneficial to the ill person adapting to a new life situation. The minister is always aware of man's ability to move toward self actualization, based on the belief of man's freedom to choose an attitude toward his life situation. Becoming involved with the ill person as he adapts requires skill in communications. Communicating involves observing and translating non-verbal communication; that is, the gestures that are seen, what is heard, the tone of voice, and general clues given through body language. Most important is facilitating an environment of acceptance by listening with an openness that conveys genuine concern. Listening to the message and understanding is vital between the pastoral visitor and the sick person, for most individuals hear only what they want to hear; therefore, the level of communication must be such that the language used is appropriate for the person involved. Clarifying thoughts and feelings to insure understanding will keep communications open. We are all in need of emotional support when faced with a crisis and those who have genuine interest in people can be a tremendous source of help. The clergy need to have an awareness of themselves with knowledge of human behavior in order to be most effective in an interpersonal relationship with another suffering human person.

Finally, the minister is always aware of his involvement with the ill person as one in which both grow from sharing in the experience. The pastoral visitor experiences the effect he may have on the ill person and also the change within himself for having been involved in the life of another person.

NOTES

1. James K. Skipper and Robert C. Leonard, "The Structural and Cultural Context of Patient Care," *Social Interaction and Patient Care* (Philadelphia: J.B. Lippincott Company, 1965), p. 232.

2. Joyce Travelbee, R.N., M.S.N., *Interpersonal Aspects of Nursing* (Philadelphia: F.A. Davis Company, 1971), p. 33.

3. Rev. Robert B. Reeves, Jr., speech to the Ohio Hospital Convention on "The Psychology of Illness," Cincinnati, Ohio, Tuesday, April 9, 1974.

4. Lisa Robinson, R.N., M.S., Ph.D., *Psychological Aspects of the Care of Hospitalized Patients* (Philadelphia: F.A. Davis Company, 2nd edition, 1973), p. 1.

5. Adrian Van Kaam, *The Art of Existential Counseling* (Wilkes-Barre, Pa.: Dimension Books, 1966), p. 93.

6. Theodore Bovet, "Attitudes Toward Suffering," *Humanitas*, Volume IX, No. 1, Duquesne University, 1973, p. 8.

7. Viktor E. Frankl, *Man's Search for Meaning* (Boston: Beacon Press, 1962), p. 114.

SELECTED BIBLIOGRAPHY

Applbaum, Ronald, *et al.*, *Fundamental Concepts of Human Communication* (San Francisco: Canfield, 1972).

Barbara, Dominick, *The Art of Listening* (Springfield: Charles C. Thomas Publishers, 1958).

Berlo, David, *The Process of Communication* (New York: Holt, Rinehart and Winston, Inc., 1960).

Birdhistell, Ray, *Kinesics and Context* (New York: Ballantine, 1972).

Dittmann, Allen, *Interpersonal Messages of Emotion* (New York: Springer Publishers, 1972).

Erikson, Erik, *Insight and Responsibility* (New York: W.W. Norton & Co., 1964).

Fast, Julius, *Body Language* (New York: M. Evans and Co., Inc., 1970).

Frankl, Viktor, *Man's Search For Meaning* (Boston: Beacon Press, 1962).

Krupar, Karen, *Communication Games* (New York: Free Press, 1973).

Ruesch, Jurgen, *Therapeutic Communication* (New York: Norton, 1973).

Schramm, Wilbur, *Human Communication: Shadow and Reality* (New York: Harper & Row, 1973).

Skipper, K. James, and Robert Leonard, *Social Interaction and Patient Care* (Philadelphia: J.B. Lippincott Co., 1965).

Speier, Matthew, *How To Observe Face to Face Communication: A Sociological Introduction* (Pacific Palisades, Cal.: Goodyear, 1973).

Van Kaam, Adrian, *Religion and Personality* (Englewood Cliffs, N.J.: Prentice Hall, 1964).

———, *Art of Existential Counseling* (Wilkes-Barre, Pa.: Dimension Books, 1966).

2. Ministering to the Sick through Prayer

A seminarian who was taking a course in clinical training in the care of the sick was confused during a pastoral visit. As he was about to conclude his visit with an elderly woman in a four-bed ward, the patient requested a prayer. He was willing to offer a prayer, but did not know what he should do about the other three patients in the room. Should he try to include them by praying very loud, or should he just ignore them and pray quietly? A religious sister who was changing her apostolate from teaching grade school children to pastoral ministry wondered, as she was making her hospital rounds, what signs the sick give to indicate they want a prayer said with them. A priest, who was growing weary of giving his blessing to each person he called on in the hospital, questioned its effectiveness being given so often.

These questions and others concerning praying with the sick are usually asked by untrained pastoral visitors. Underlying them are two more basic questions: When should the pastoral care person pray with the sick, and secondly, what type of prayer should be offered when a prayer is appropriate? In this chapter I will attempt to answer these questions and express other ideas concerning the ministry of praying with the sick.

When To Pray with the Sick

Jesus believed it was possible to commune with God through prayer. He did it, and yet did not tell his followers when they should pray. He left this for man to determine considering the many varying circumstances of his life. However, one situation in which a person commonly turns to prayer is the sickroom, yet often he finds it very difficult to pray under these conditions because his mind is occupied with his illness or because he is unaccustomed to praying.

So frequently the sick person calls upon the minister to assist him in the art of praying, of communicating with God. Here the pastoral person attempts to unite the patient with God. In order to do this, the minister needs to know God and the sick person. This presumes, then, that the pastoral visitor is a person of prayer and has a deep relationship with God. It also presumes that he knows the patient and his individual needs.

Thus the contents of the prayer in the sickroom are like the contents of the patient's food tray, tailor-made to fit his needs. Steak smothered in onions and french fried potatoes are not given to a person the first few days following the removal of his gallbladder. Rather he is served a clear liquid diet consisting of broth and tea because these liquids will best aid this patient in recovering from this type of surgery. A similar approach is used with prayer in the sickroom. It is tailor-made to fit the individual person and his condition because the minister knows his patient, the degree of his illness, something of his emotional stability, and most important, the degree of his relationship to God.[1]

For some people, prayer is like an aspirin. They use it whenever they have problems and never at any other time. Others love prayer superficially, the way they love poetry and music. It's beautiful and soothing to listen to, but there is no real communication between them and their God. Others never pray at all because they profess not to believe in any kind of personal God.

Others have prayed in the past, but have stopped because of some tragedy in their lives. Perhaps they hate God because they blame him for the death of their innocent little child. Others pray sometimes, but expect the minister always to pray when he visits them. The elderly Irish Catholic lady, for example, expects a blessing every time the priest comes to see her and indicates this by making the sign of the cross as the priest is preparing to leave. Finally, there are others who have an intimate relationship with God. They pray frequently and attend the eucharistic celebration daily.

Obviously for some of these people any kind of prayer will be out of place because the persons are not ready for it yet and maybe never will be during the present sickness. For others, one kind of prayer will be suitable while another will not meet their needs at all. So it is out of place for a pastoral person to pray very loud in a ward in an attempt to include three or four patients in a prayer.

In order for the pastoral visitor to be effective, he has to gain insight into the patient and be flexible to adjust to each individual person. This cannot be done if he has the attitude that it is part of his job to impart his blessing or offer a prayer with each and every patient he visits. When a minister has this approach, it seems that he is filling his own need and not the patient's. Another difficulty with this attitude is that prayer with every visit can easily become generalized and superficial.

On the other hand the pastoral person cannot do what is best for the individual patient if he has the policy of never praying with the sick unless a direct request is made. This seems like a mature manner of dealing with an adult patient except that some people don't have the courage to ask for a prayer, others never ask because they presume that a prayer will be offered without a request being made, and others feel they have no right to ask since they are not a member of his denomination or church. It's best, then, for the minister not to have any absolute rule of always praying or never praying. Rather he should take the approach of praying with the sick (to answer the first question) when the patient directly or indirectly asks for it and when a prayer flows naturally from the pastoral conversation.

At times the patient will directly request a prayer at the conclusion of the visit. At other times the patient will indirectly ask for a prayer by folding his hands, bowing his head, or prepare to make the sign of the cross as the priest is about to leave. These are clear indications that the patient wants and expects his minister to help him communicate with God. At still other times, prayer seems to be a natural conclusion of the pastoral conversation. The sick person may indicate his need for prayer by casually speaking of the difficulty he is experiencing in his attempts to pray. Or perhaps, the person relates his history of illness during the last several months, mentioning the many operations and painful procedures he has undergone in his unsuccessful attempts to be healed and that now it's simply in God's hands. In situations like this, it seems natural for the pastoral person to intercede for the sick by calling upon the divine physician for assistance.

The Type of Prayer To Be Offered

It is presumed that the prayer in the sickroom will monopolize the attention of the minister and the patient. This cannot be done if the clergyman is distracted by his own personal concerns or is nervous, hurried or too conscious of the physical conditions of the room. By his own concentration the pastoral visitor attracts the sick person's attention, even amid adverse conditions, i.e., the patient's roommate playing the radio or the patient being in an oxygen tent. However, in order to sustain the sick person's attention and to answer the second question concerning the type of prayer to be offered, the following four guidelines are suggested.

First, it's important to have a few seconds of quiet before the prayer to allow the pastoral person time to collect his thoughts and for the patient to put other things out of his mind. This brief period of quiet in the beginning, in addition to a pause during the prayer, also gives the Holy Spirit time to work through the minister and in the sick person.

Second, the prayer is brief. The sick room is rarely a good place for a long oratorical prayer because the patient is often weak, and a long prayer will only tire him. In addition, the pastoral visitor keeps the prayer brief out of consideration for the other patients in the room who may be keeping quiet out of respect for God and religion during the prayer.

Third, it's good to insert the person's name in the prayer. Our parishes, hospitals, and the world in general are becoming more and more impersonal because of the great numbers of people and the speed of our day. By placing the patient's name in the prayer, the minister conveys that the sick person is not forgotten in the masses of people, but that he is an individual about whom the pastoral visitor is concerned.

Fourth, the prayer has application, that is, the prayer recognizes the sick person's needs and expresses his yearnings and desires.[2]

A few examples would be helpful in explaining fully the meaning of application and the difference between a good and a poor application. A middle-aged lady was admitted to the hospital for severe burns which she felt were caused because her doctor gave her too many x-ray treatments on her legs and arms in an attempt to cure a skin rash. For the first few days the lady was filled with anger at her doctor and was not ready to forgive him. She ventilated this anger to the minister and at the end of the visit asked him to say a prayer. He prayed, "O Jesus, you appeared to your followers that first Easter Sunday evening and wished peace to them because they were very upset. Mrs. Jones is upset this evening. She feels she has been hospitalized because of her physician's mistake. We beg you, Lord, to instill in her heart a sense of peace, a sense that you accept her with her angry feelings toward her doctor. We ask this in Jesus' name. Amen." This prayer has good application because it touches the lady where she is. A prayer for forgiveness for her physician at this time was out of place because she was not ready for it yet.

In a pastoral visit a young mother who was dying of cancer expressed intense anxiety for her three small children. She feared that they would greatly miss a mother's love in growing up. The pastoral person concluded his visit with the prayer, "Lord, many times you enjoyed taking little children in your arms and blessing them. On one occasion you were even tired and your apostles discouraged the children from coming to you, but you wanted them to come anyway because of your intense love for them. We trust, Lord, that because of your love for little ones you will take a special interest in Mrs. Brown's three small children, helping them as they encounter problems in growing up. Amen." The minister could have offered a prayer emphasizing God's forgiveness of her sins, but this would have been a poor application because that was not the mother's main concern and because that could easily have led her to believe that God was punishing her for her sins.

In both of these examples, good application was achieved by summarizing the conversation with the patient. This summarizing is similar to that which the pastoral counselor does at the conclusion of a counseling session. In his summation of the pastoral visit, the minister is specific and emphasizes the individual's "hot spot," that is, the subject matter which the patient shared with the greatest emotion. After a lengthy conversation a pastor might mention several things in prayer which the person has been discussing, but omit the subject material which was most important (that which contained the greatest feeling). Of course, this is a poor application of prayer and does not fill the patient's needs.[3]

It is also poor application for a minister to limit his prayers to those of petition because good application means touching the person where he is. Sometimes a patient has recovered from serious surgery and is ready to go back home. A prayer of thanksgiving and praise of God often expresses his feelings at this point. Another patient has spent a half an hour telling the pastoral person all of the sins of his life and how sorry he is for them. In such a situation a prayer of sorrow and a reassurance of God's mercy are appropriate.

A final note concerning the application of prayer is that it should have reasonable limits. A prayer to free the post-surgical patient from all pain is simply unrealistic. A better approach in such a situation is to reassure him of God's special care of the sick and ask God to give him the strength of Christ as he suffered on the cross.

In emphasizing that the prayer in the sickroom should be tailor-made to fit the patient's needs and that it should have good application, spontaneous prayers have been encouraged. Yet, this does not rule out the possibility of the effectiveness of using formulas or memorized prayers. Undoubtedly, there are occasions when a formula is more appropriate than a spontaneous prayer. Sometimes when a person has been away from the Church and prayer for a long time, the Our Father is the best prayer to offer because he has forgotten the words to it. Maybe that night the former active Catholic will pray the Our Father now that he has been helped to remember the words. For dying people the most beneficial prayers are often the Our Father, the Hail Mary, and a couple of ejaculations. And for others who have a special liking for Sacred Scripture or have a need for reassurance, perhaps the most effective prayer is the 23rd Psalm.

There is a place in the modern sickroom for the priestly blessing. After all, it is a sacramental, and many people, especially the aged, value it highly. It seems too that the priestly blessing would make a natural conclusion to any prayer the priest offers. This doesn't mean though that he would necessarily use it every time he prays or visits the sick.

In conclusion, the pastoral care person is open to the Holy Spirit when he is visiting the sick and does not have any set policy. He adjusts to each situation and allows the Spirit to guide him to meet the sick person's need and not his own in regard to praying or not praying, and in regard to the type of prayer that is offered when one is indicated.

NOTES

1. Rev. Wayne E. Oates, *An Introduction to Pastoral Counseling*, Broadman Press, Nashville, Tenn., 1959, pp. 212-213.
2. Richard D. Cabot and Russel L. Dicks, *Art of Ministering to the Sick*, Macmillan, New York, 1936, p. 220.
3. "A Dynamic Concept of Praying For The Sick," *Pastoral Psychology*, October 1969, Vol. 20, No. 197, p. 45.

SELECTED BIBLIOGRAPHY

Autton, Normand, ed., *Manual of Prayers and Readings with the Sick* (New York: Morehouse, 1970).
Bassett, Bernard, *Let's Start Praying Again* (New York: Doubleday, 1973).
Drescher, John, *Blessings By Your Bedside* (Scottdale, Pa.: Herald Press, 1969).
Evely, Louis, *Our Prayer* (New York: Seabury, 1970).

Hinnebusch, Paul, *Prayer: The Search For Authenticity* (New York: Sheed & Ward, 1969).

Johnson, Paul, *Psychology of Pastoral Care* (New York: Abingdon Press, 1953).

McEvoy, Hubert, S.J., *In Times of Sickness* (Springfield, Ill.: Templegate Press, 1962).

National Association of Catholic Chaplains, *Fear Not, I Am With You* (Staten Island, N.Y.: Alba House, 1970).

Nouwen, Henry, *With Open Hands* (Notre Dame, Ind.: Ave Maria, 1972).

Rahner, Karl, *On Prayer* (Paramus, New Jersey: Paulist Press, 1968).

Scherzer, Carl, *Ministering to the Physically Sick* (Philadelphia: Fortress Press, 1968).

Westberg, Granger, *Minister and Doctor Meet* (New York: Harper & Row, 1961).

3. Ministering to the Sick through the Sacraments

All three of the major automobile companies announced in 1974 that they sold less cars than in the previous year and consequently made less profit. Like most industries, these companies rate their success by the number of products they sell and the money they make. Thus the emphasis is on quantity.

Sometimes the Church uses the same standard for success, and sacramental effectiveness is rated by quantity i.e., the number of Communions distributed and anointings given. The Church can learn many things from business, but how to measure the effectiveness of sacramental ministration is not one of them. The fact that priests slip quickly in and out of hospital rooms to dispense the sacraments in a cold mechanical way is evidence of the influence this standard of measurement has on their ministry. Another influence is an excessive emphasis on the principle *"ex opere operato"* which dictates that the sacraments are almost a kind of magical rite, producing grace without any effort on the part of the recipient or the minister of the sacrament. In reality, just the opposite is true because the sacraments are signs of grace and of faith; they are not things, but actions: encounters with the risen Lord.[1] Fr. Bernard Haring expressed a similar concept to the priests of Springfield, Illinois saying that the sacraments are outstanding and privileged signs of God's presence with his people and furthermore are signs of hope, graciousness, love and justice. In order that the sacraments become these meaningful signs for the people, Fr. Haring concludes that the heart of the minister needs to be filled with faith, joy and thanksgiving.[2]

This does not mean that the actions of the Holy Spirit are

bound to these seven signs and that he cannot act through others. It simply means that these are the normal ways in which God manifests himself, but he is not confined to them. God is active in our world daily but it is often hidden and veiled. Human beings need the sacraments at specific times when God's presence is made explicit through signs like bread, wine and oil. The sacraments are privileged moments of his presence when the faithful celebrate explicitly the presence of God in their midst. Thus the first and basic principle concerning sacramental pastoral care of the sick is: the sacraments are outstanding and privileged moments of encountering God, but are not the only ones.

The ministry of Christ was a healing ministry of restoring the whole person to health, not just one of being concerned with the body or the soul. Many times Christ healed the whole person, i.e., curing the paralytic of his disease as well as forgiving him his sins. In imitation of Christ, the Church's ministry is not to souls but to people. Thus her ministry is not confined to the life to come, but also a ministry which attempts to put together the broken pieces of human lives. Formerly, the Church viewed man in a fragmented manner, dividing him into body and soul. This indicated the Greek influence in the Church, dissecting man into parts. The biblical view though, looks upon man as a whole integrated person who is not divided into body and soul. This leads to the second principle: sacraments are not for souls only, but for the whole person.[3]

According to the *Constitution On the Liturgy* (No. 42) the visitation of the sick is the duty of all Christians who share in the concern and love of Christ and urges them to strengthen the sick in the Lord by offering them help as brothers and sisters. By their presence and concern they support the sick person in his pain and help to relieve his loneliness. Through the involvement of the community in the pastoral care of the sick they are fulfilling the words of Jesus—"I was sick and you visited me." The Constitution further stresses that the liturgical services are never private functions but are celebrations of the whole Church. So whenever it is possible the faithful, especially the relatives and friends of the sick person, are invited to be present to share in the administration of the sacrament by becoming actively involved in the rites. This community concept of sacraments is applied to all the sacraments since there is no such thing as a private sacrament. It means a drastic reversal from the previous custom of anointing someone privately with no member of the community present. When Holy Communion is given to the sick, the new ritual *Rite of Anointing and Pastoral Care of the Sick* urges the whole family to partake of the Bread of Life to signify the unity of all those concerned for the sick person. When Catholics refer to the Eucharist only as the real presence of Christ, they miss the fuller meaning St. Paul refers to when he says, "We are all joined in a single body because we all share in the one bread."[5] In addition to the involvement of relatives and friends, the sacraments are administered communally, if possible. So when two or more people in the same area are to be anointed or receive Communion, an attempt is made to bring them to a common room so that the community nature of the sacraments is emphasized. The third principle, then, is that the care of the sick is the concern of the whole Christian community. These three principles have a tremendous influence on how the sacraments are celebrated for the sick. The acceptance or rejection of these principles by the priest and faithful determines pastoral practice—the manner in which they celebrate the sacraments.[6]

Holy Communion

In the new ritual a greeting and penitential rite similar to that at the beginning of the Eucharistic liturgy introduces the Communion service and a brief reading from Sacred Scripture follows. These prayers help to stir up the faith of the recipients. After the distribution of Communion which is immediately preceded by the same prayer as at Mass ("This is the Lamb of God . . ."), a final prayer begging God for healing concludes the service.

It is impossible for the priest to offer all these prayers when he distributes Communion in large nursing homes and hospitals. There is simply not sufficient time to do this. However, the priest does take enough time to stimulate the faith of the sick by offering at least some brief prayer before Communion similar to that preceding the distribution at Mass.

It is of little value for many patients for the priest to rush into a room and say, "Body of Christ" and rush out again because they don't have time to turn off their television or radio and generally lack the opportunity to prepare to receive Communion and consider their thanksgiving. When the priest rushes in distributing Communion, he creates a lack of reverence for the sacraments among the personnel who say to themselves, "Why should we show any reverence for Communion when the priest doesn't?" One lady who received Communion from a priest whose attitude was "quick-in, quick-out" said, "It doesn't even seem like I'm receiving anything special." A seventeen-year-old girl who received Communion from another priest whose attitude was, "Let's make this a meaningful encounter with Christ" commented, "I receive Communion here in the hospital just like I do at Mass."

In order to avoid rushing on Communion rounds and to enable the sacrament to be distributed reverently to many sick people in large health facilities, the chaplain enlists the aid of religious sisters and lay people. After a brief course preparing them to be extra-ordinary ministers of Communion, they administer the sacrament well and allow all the patients to have a meaningful encounter with Christ because sufficient time is given to each patient. In addition, by having extra-ordinary ministers the chaplain is involving more of the community in the care of the sick.

Holy Communion is distributed to the sick in large health facilities in several ways today. Some chaplains carry the Blessed Sacrament with them during their routine visitation and at its conclusion ask the patient if he wishes to receive Communion. If the person wants to receive, the minister reverently lays the pyx on the table and begins the prayers. Some ministers find this method very efficient and acceptable while others are uneasy about carrying the Blessed Sacrament with them for several hours, so they visit the patients first, noting those who wish to receive Communion and then return later for its distribution.

Some Catholic health facilities still have the practice of bringing Communion in the early morning. This is a very quiet time, but often the patients are asleep or fall back to sleep immediately after receiving Communion. The more common custom seems to be to distribute Communion in the evening after visiting hours are over. The chaplain assists the patients in their preparation with night prayers over the loudspeaker. In concluding his prayers the chaplain reminds the patients who plan to receive our Lord to make their own private preparation. Finally, some Catholic health facilities have daily Mass on closed circuit television every afternoon and immediately after the Mass the ministers of the Eucharist go to the rooms to distribute Communion. By distributing in this manner there is a beautiful connection between the Eucharistic Sacrificial Meal and the patients' reception of Communion.

The new ritual (No. 27) reiterates the importance of viaticum. As the Christian is dying, he is strengthened with the Bread of Life which is a pledge of the resurrection Christ promised. "He who feeds on my flesh and drinks my blood has life eternal and I will raise him up on the last day."[7] A dying person is often not able to receive the whole host and appreciates it if the minister gives him only a small particle, followed by a spoon of water. If the patient is afflicted with a disease which interferes with his ability to swallow, the minister may consider giving him Communion under the species of the Precious Blood.

Receiving Communion means many different things to various sick people. For some, it is just something you do daily when you're sick in a hospital, while for others it has a deep significance. It means they are not in this big strange hospital alone—Jesus is with them; it gives them a feeling of confidence that somehow everything will be okay; it helps them to pour out their deepest fears and frustrations to a Person who understands, cares and will assist them with their difficulties.

Recently, I witnessed a beautiful example of the value of Communion for a young hospitalized lady whose baby had died shortly after birth. Her husband and her mother were in the room comforting her, and it was evident that this common loss had drawn them closer together. Their union was deepened when all of them were united to Christ by receiving our Lord during the evening Communion rounds and surely our Lord joined them in supporting each other.

Anointing of the Sick

In the past many Catholics were frightened by the visit of the priest when they became sick because they associated the priest with "last rites" and death. The Second Vatican Council attempted to clarify the understanding of Extreme Unction by saying that it is more fitting to call it the Anointing of the Sick. The "last rites" really is Communion for a dying person. Anointing is not the last sacrament, but rather a sacrament for the person who has become seriously ill. The Second Vatican Council says, "As soon as anyone of the faithful begins to be in danger of death from sickness or old age, the appropriate time for him to receive this sacrament has certainly already arrived."[8]

The Bishops' Committee on the Liturgy explains in some detail who is entitled to receive the anointing. It urges Catholics to gain a proper understanding of the sacrament by referring to the epistle of James and explains that Christians seriously ill from sickness or old age are the proper recipients of the sacrament. It suggests that the priest is not to be scrupulous in this matter and enumerates the kinds of people to be anointed: "In concrete terms, patients undergoing major surgery, the elderly debilitated by old age, children who have reached the age of reason (that is, who have sufficient understanding to be comforted by this sacrament) and are seriously ill certainly qualify for this sacrament. The seriously sick who have lost consciousness or the use of reason should be anointed if they would have requested it were they in command of their faculties. The sacrament may also be repeated in the course of the same illness, not only if the sick person suffers a relapse after a period of convalescence, as was already permitted, but even if in the course of the same sickness, his condition becomes more critical."[9]

The revised rite also moves away from a quasi-private ceremony and prefers a communal celebration which is normally celebrated with the sick person's relatives and friends present, actively participating by reading, singing, etc. Thus the Anointing of the Sick is not administered in a mechanistic manner but rather as a sacrament of the community of faith. After all, this sacrament as St. James says in his epistle[10] presumes faith which is important for the minister of the sacrament and more important for the recipient. For the sick man is saved by his faith and the faith of the Christian community which remembers the death and resurrection of Christ and looks forward to sharing the joy of heaven with the creator.

The new rite further illustrates the pertinent effects of the sacrament for the sick. Often a sick person experiences bodily pain, psychic depression and isolation from his usual routine as well as from normal society. He tends to become impatient, sulky, excessively preoccupied with self, depressed, and may experience spiritual dryness. To counteract this, the anointing not only directs its energies toward a spiritual salvation which is achieved in death and toward a bodily healing which occurs in complete recovery, but directs its main thrust at the specific obstacles to growth and salvation arising from the sickness. As a result, the anointing with the Holy Spirit received with faith heals the ailing Christian either by removing the external cause of this danger that is the sickness itself, or by imparting a special strength to his entire being so that he can bear up under the illness. In other words, the anointing enables the Christian in spite of and through his illness to follow and identify with the suffering and risen Lord.[11] These effects are more clearly evident from the new form of the anointing: "Through this holy anointing and his great love for you, may the Lord help you by the power of his Holy Spirit. R. Amen. May the Lord who freed you from sin heal you and extend his saving grace to you. R. Amen."[12]

Baptism

The final sacrament that is frequently administered in a hospital is Baptism. Ideally, this sacrament is received in the parish church where the Christian community accepts a new member into their midst. Ideally too, the parents take an active part in the administration of the sacrament and are reminded that their Christian faith at this time supplies for the inability of the child to express his faith in Christ's redeeming love and also of their obligation to foster the seed of faith implanted in their child through the sacrament by their example and instruction.

However, when an infant of Catholic parentage is in real danger of dying, he is baptized at the hospital and later, if the child survives, the other ceremonies are supplied at the church. Yet even in an emergency baptism in a hospital, if circumstances permit, the parents are invited to witness the baptism, hear the priest or nurse offer a brief prayer before pouring the water, and also make a profession of faith since it is into this faith the parents wish the child baptized. Thus every effort is made to remove any mechanical, magical concept of a sacrament and to make the sacrament a real meeting with God.

A young couple who were informed by the pediatrician that their two-day-old daughter could not live because of a serious malfunctioning heart requested the chaplain to baptize their child. This couple who had a deep desire to have a baby were very upset because of the impending loss of their daughter. As the hours wore on in the hospital room they struggled to find some peace and asked the common questions, "Why did this happen to us? Why did God allow this?" They were assisted in this struggle by encountering Christ in a meaningful rite of baptism for their daughter. Nothing could take away the pain from the couple, but it was evident that they were comforted by the fact that their daughter who was just initiated into the Christian faith would be initiated into the heavenly community after her death.

Formerly, all the nurses working in Catholic hospitals were

instructed soon after employment how to baptize and informed that it was their duty to baptize all dying infants, even if this was against the parents' wishes. Some Catholic hospitals in our country still continue this practice, believing that because of the baptism the infant is saved from being sent to limbo. When this practice is reviewed in the light of the Second Vatican Council, it is clearly opposed to the principles of ecumenism. In addition, the faith and discipline of the Church do not demand that all dying infants be baptized, lest they be excluded from heaven.[13] This unfortunate practice arose in the Church because of an excessive emphasis on the power of sin, in spite of the fact that Paul in his letter to the Romans indicates the supreme saving power of Christ's death and resurrection over sin: "Therefore, just as through one man sin entered into the world and with sin death, death thus coming to all men inasmuch as all sinned. But the gift is not like the offense. For if by the offense of the one man all died, much more did the grace of God, and the gracious gift of the one man, Jesus Christ, abound for all."[14]

So the chaplain or a nurse baptizes only the infants in critical condition whose parents wish the child baptized and relies on God in his own merciful way, which he has not made known to mankind, to save those who die without baptism. The personnel at the hospital keep in mind that the sacraments are the normal but not the only channels of salvation.

Conclusion

To follow Jesus when everything is going well is easy, but when he speaks of suffering, of enduring misunderstandings and of experiencing spiritual dryness, then clouds appear and the going gets tough. Precisely at this time, the Christian is like Peter, James and John crying out for some tangible evidence that the risk of totally following Christ is really worth it. In these difficult moments a Christian wants some tangible proof that enduring all this is worthwhile; he wants a transfiguration like Christ gave to Peter, James and John to support his faith.

These painful moments demand a deep faith to hear the Father speaking to us through the clouds and urging us to continue our commitment to Christ, to continue believing in Christ without any absolute proof. However, the ordinary Christian receives a tangible awareness of Jesus, both God and Man, in his risen glory, by participating fully in the sacraments. These are his gifts to his disciples today which make myriad repetitions of the historical transfiguration unnecessary for frequent and fervent reception of the sacraments sustains the faith of the Christian.[15]

Every experience, including the experience of sickness and suffering, is an opportunity for growth. In fact, during sickness people are more open to grow than at any other times in their lives. Pastoral persons have great opportunities to help the sick take advantage of this, but how often do they? Possibly one reason is that currently pastoral persons are taking workshops and courses in counseling and psychology and are not emphasizing prayer in their own personal lives or striving to learn the art of prayer. Thus in visiting the sick they use their counseling skills frequently, but do not integrate this with a skill of communicating God to their patients.[16]

Today, people are screaming to talk to someone about God, heaven, faith and prayer. This was clearly evidenced recently when Fr. Edward Farrell, a professor at Sacred Heart Seminary and the author of two books on "prayer," spoke in Cincinnati, Ohio on the topic *Prayer is Hunger.* His lecture, sponsored by the Religious Education Department of the Cincinnati Archdiocesan School Office, was attended by over 1100 religious and lay people who were eager to learn how to improve their communication with God. Audiences of this size indicate modern man's deep yearning to attain a more intimate relationship with God. Hopefully, the pastoral person will equip himself with skills both in counseling and in communicating with God so that he can take full advantage of the openness of the sick to grow in many different ways through the experience of sickness.

One hospital team ministry composed of a religious sister and a priest spend about fifteen minutes in shared prayers of petition for the sick before beginning their visits. Certainly these two pastoral persons, integrating counseling with the spiritual, are prepared to meet the overall needs of their patients and not just their emotional or counseling needs.

NOTES

1. Rev. Eugene Selzer, "Sacraments and Healing," *The Updated Chaplaincy* (Workshop Proceedings), The Catholic Hospital Association, St. Louis, Missouri, 1973, p. 58.
2. Rev. Bernard Haring, "Evangelization," *Continuing Education for Priests*, Springfield, Illinois, July 15, 1974.
3. Selzer, *op. cit.*, p. 57.
4. Matthew 25:36.
5. 1 Corinthians 10:17.
6. Selzer, *op. cit.*, p. 58.
7. John 6:54.
8. *Constitution on the Sacred Liturgy*, December 4, 1963, n. 73.
9. *Study Text II—Anointing and Pastoral Care of the Sick*, United States Catholic Conference, 1973, p. 10.
10. James 5:15.
11. *Study Test II—Anointing and Pastoral Care of the Sick*, *op. cit.*, pp. 24-25.
12. *Rite of Anointing and Pastoral Care of the Sick*, n. 76.
13. Rev. Lawrence Landini, O.F.M., "To Baptize or Not To Baptize," Archdiocesan Association of Catholic Chaplains, Dayton, Ohio, January 23, 1973.
14. Romans 5:12, 15.
15. Rev. Ralph J. Sehlinger, O.P., "Editorial," *Cross and Crown*, September 1974, Vol. 26, No. 3, pp. 228-229.
16. Rev. James J. Gill, S.J., "Accountability and the Chaplain," Ninth Annual Convention of the National Association of Catholic Chaplains, Hyannis, Massachusetts, September 18, 1974.

4. Ministering to Obstetrical and Gynecological Patients

In Western culture marriage is contracted by a couple who for various reasons unique to their relationship desire to live together and raise a family. The concept of family varies with cultures. In this society the nuclear family is most familiar, consisting of a man and a woman with their children. There are many reasons for couples to choose marriage as a way of life, economic, social status, sexual attraction, and love. It is hoped that a marriage is based on mature love, shared with the beloved and nurtured through respect for one another. Erich Fromm explains, that "genuine love is an expression of productiveness and implies care, respect, responsibility and knowledge. It is not an "affect" in the sense of being affected by somebody, but an active striving for growth and happiness of the loved person, rooted in one's own capacity to love."[1] Only the man who loves himself with respect and values his life can adequately give love to another.

A couple living an interdependent life, committed to enhance each other's personal growth as well as their own growth, will want to create new life as an extension of their love and strengthen their oneness as a unit. When a child is born into a family that has love to give, it will be received as a joyous event. The parents will have prepared themselves to assume the new roles demanded by the arrival of a child. As parenthood is the most important responsibility facing the couple, they will experience normal apprehensions in handling the infant and in caring for its needs. They are conscious of their need to be good parents. Society expects them to nurture and guide their children to become mature persons, capable of loving others as they love themselves.

Couples, during the pregnancy, who understand the importance of parenting, will discuss with each other their role concepts and together anticipate parenthood. They attend classes for expectant parents, learn how to care for the infant, and possibly get involved in child rearing seminars. These couples are aware that they have some knowledge of parenting from their own life experience of growing up. The woman learns mothering from her own mother, imitating her as she was nurtured from infancy toward adulthood. The man learns that mother takes care of the child and that father is the protector. In today's society the movement is toward both parents wanting to become involved in caring for the infant and to share the responsibility. An infant born into this kind of atmosphere will experience warmth and acceptance, and have an opportunity to grow up in a family, the basic unit of society. This is where a child learns he is valued, worthwhile and loved. He learns how to interact within the family system, and transfers this to communicating outside the family.

Parents and the Maternity Unit

A pastoral person visiting the maternity unit needs to be perceptive of the mother's feelings and hear how they are experiencing their life situations. He may hear the concerns of a young mother about being a "good mother." She is expressing some anxieties about her new responsibility. He may want to say, "You will do fine," or "Things will be all right, once you get home," or some similar remark. Actually she needs to verbalize her feelings to someone who will listen to her. Listening is an art in which every spiritual leader needs to develop skill. Listening with an openness to the other person, as the "other," hearing from his frame of reference, without distorting what is being said is of upmost importance. This involves hearing with empathy as described by Travelbee: "One shares in the psychological state of another but not to the extent of thinking and feeling as the other person. To empathize is to 'share' in, but to stand apart from, the object of one's empathy. This 'apartness' in empathy does not imply a cold objectivity; rather it implies a sense of sharing while being detached from the object of one's empathy."[2] The religious will be supportive to a mother just by listening empathetically and responding in an understanding manner.

The minister can give reassurance positively by having knowledge of the normal acquaintance process that takes place between the mother and her infant. During pregnancy the mother shared a closeness to her developing infant as she carried it; she had fantasies about the sex, how it would look and be. After birth, her infant is a reality; her fantasy becomes real. She begins to feel him now in a skin to skin touching; getting to know each other. Montagu explains "that during the birth process mother and infant have had a somewhat trying time. At birth each clearly requires the reassurance of the other's presence. The reassurance for the mother lies in the sight of her baby, its first cry, and in its closeness to her body. For the baby it consists in the contact with and warmth of the mother's body, the support in her cradled arms, the caressing it receives and the suckling at her breast, the welcome into the bosom of the family."[3]

If her husband was with her throughout labor and delivery they have experienced the joy together. The minister supports them as he shares their joy. When the couple are separated during the labor and delivery the new father needs encouragement. He needs to know that gradually he will develop a closeness when fondling and caring for his infant, and that the father-child relationship will grow. The pastor recognizes the joy and apprehension felt by new couples and understands that at this time they need reassurance in their changing roles.

Immature Parents

Marriage which is contracted because of a pregnancy can be a traumatic experience. The inability of the couple to interact with each other as persons causes them to experience turmoil and frustration. In addition, their relationship lacks the stability necessary in rearing a family. The pregnancy may have been planned by the young woman to force the marriage. Or the young man may feel a deep obligation to marry and give his child a home. The parents of the couple involved can also force the marriage to prevent an out of wedlock child. Developing a relationship and preparing for the new baby can be very difficult, but with proper counseling the young couple can learn to know each other. This depends on their honesty and in having an openness for growth. A minister aware of such a relationship should make every effort to counsel the couple and if more intense therapy is needed to get them involved in regular sessions with a family therapist.

The arrival of an infant into an immature relationship can be a disaster, causing a disruption, because neither parent is mature enough to accept the responsibility of parenthood. Role changes from husband to father and wife to mother become indistinguishable since both have not established their own identity as persons. This is seen among adolescent couples who have not worked through their adolescent identity crisis.

Immature couples who marry in hopes that their partners will fulfill their needs and expectations suffer deep frustrations. They experience disappointment in their partner, feeling rejection. Because of their inability to accept the other as a unique person, they are unable to bridge the communication gap. Because of their inability to feel love and security within themselves, they are unable to give love. They are unable to cope with the differences in each other and establish any kind of deep relationship necessary for mutual growth. Virginia Satir describes this as, "the couple discover after marriage that the other is 'different,' from what each expected during courtship, they become disillusioned and that their differentness seems to take away from each other rather than add to them so they see each other in a new light."[4] These parents are unable to accept the interdependency of the marital relationship and counseling is necessary for them to develop a mature way of coping as a unit.

The pastoral counselor needs to assist each one to gain insight into the behavior that inhibits the experiencing of happiness. Loving, respecting and viewing themselves as worthwhile individuals can be developed with consistent encounters and a willing clergyman who understands human behavior. Assisting couples to become mature individuals, to accept each other and the responsibility of parenthood can be most rewarding. The minister becomes a very important person in helping couples view life more realistically. Mature, independent adults view their marital relationships as a complementary role. Each contributes to the life of the other, developing a close union in which children feel loved and valued. Evoy and O'Keefe say, "the unity of the man and the woman in complementing love is brought about by psychologically sharing with each other all that they are. Everything in each person is entrusted to the other."[5]

Immature couples are unable to complement each other because of the need for the self esteem and love necessary as the basis for developing a mature relationship. A child entering the family unit of immature parents is an interference and results in the disruption of the empathetic relationship the infant should experience with his parents. Harry Stack Sullivan says that, "Anxiety relates to the whole field of interpersonal interaction; that is, anxiety about anything in the mother induces anxiety in the infant."[6]

The spiritual leader who listens empathetically will be aware of the distress felt by the mother who feels disappointment in her husband whom she expected to give her security. She may remark, "He's supposed to know that," "All husbands do that," or "My father always did it that way, why can't my husband?" The husband remarks that, "All women are supposed to know how to take care of a baby," or "It is her job to rear the children. I work and bring home the money," or "That's what my mother always did," or some such remark that indicates the level of maturity. Many young parents try to live their marital lives by the learned behavior of their own parents' relationship.

The wife soon learns, if she is striving toward maturity, that her husband is not her father nor the ideal male she fantasized in her dreams. The husband learns that his wife is not his mother and she is not the woman of his fantasy world. When both accept this and begin to view each other as unique persons, their relationship begins to develop into a deep friendship and love, and is shared with the children.

It may be that one or the other cannot recognize immaturity or is unable to let go of old patterns of behavior. This results in dysfunctional parenting. They need to be encouraged by the religious counselor to view themselves as having a very valuable part in childrearing. The father who feels insecure in his role by trying to maintain some sort of "male image," needs assistance in viewing himself as having an important role in childrearing. He needs to understand that children learn by what they see and feel, not by words. They know when they are loved. The pastoral person needs to have some understanding of communication skills and family systems.

Most couples seek the assistance of their minister when major difficulties arise that make life intolerable. They will open up readily to a religious counselor who shows genuine concern for them. They trust him and believe that he has the answers to their dilemma, and thus the clergy of today must be aware of the psychosocial aspects of family life. Each family is unique with its own rules and laws and methods of interacting. Developing oneself as a helping person in the lives of those seeking assistance requires knowledge of self and the ability to view humans as unique. Listening openly, trying to enter into another's world, to understand the meaning life has for them, requires skill. Van Kaam describes the counselor's relationship to the counselee as responding to the other authentically in therapeutic caring, "The very trust which I give without limits to my client, revealed in my unconditional therapeutic care, is in and by itself an appeal to the counselee to be concerned as I am concerned,"[7] which enables the other person to be responsible for his own destiny. Ministers who view man as unique, having dignity and the freedom to choose, will develop relationships that allow the finding of meaning in life situations enabling movement toward self actualization.

Parents are willing to give their children their best. When they seek guidance, the pastoral person uses every possible means to assist them in their goal—to become better persons. A knowledgeable spiritual leader who recognizes his own limitations refers the family to a family therapist when he realizes the need for more indepth therapy.

In the hospital environment the nurse does not always hear the distress clues of the mother because her orientation is directed toward giving mothers physical care. Little time is spent in perceiving psychosocial problems unless these problems present themselves as behavior problems, i.e., depression, anger, isolation, etc. Nurses in some maternity units develop a relationship with the parents during pregnancy. After delivery they help the parents through their adjustment process, either as new parents or for the addition of another child. The nurse can share valuable information with the religious leader when he makes the initial contact with the mother of the family on the unit. She will recognize the value of the minister and will co-operate with him to meet the total needs of her client.

Parents Who Have Difficulty Accepting Their Child

In some hospitals the minister is very much a part of the health team. The nurses refer women to him when they recognize that a mother may be experiencing difficulties. Occasionally a nurse will have a mother who refuses to see her baby. This mother should be referred to the religious counselor. The reasons for her resentment or inability to accept her child may be varied and very complex. She may be angry because she did not want the child but was unable to go through with an abortion and continued to full term. She needs to verbalize her feelings and thoughts concerning herself as a person. She may have had poor mother-child relationships in her own life resulting in a fear of her own ability to function adequately as a mother. Her low self esteem may inhibit her from viewing her life situation positively and with the added new responsibility she may be unable to function. She may resent the baby if she has an unsatisfactory husband-wife relationship which will place the burden of rearing the child totally on her.

Couples who are having difficulties within their marriage sometimes will have a child in hopes that their marriage will become more stable. This is a disaster as a child adds responsibility to an already unstable relationship and the infant becomes a pawn to be used by both partners. It may also cause a marriage to disintegrate leaving the mother and child alone. The infant will be an intrusion in a marriage where the husband is content only with his wife. He needs her total love and companionship and is unable to share her with a child. He may reject the child completely or both by deserting the family. The inability of immature husbands to share their wife's love stems for unmet love needs in their own childhood. The responsibility of parenthood is overwhelming and they are unable to cope adequately. Ann complained that her husband insisted that she give him all her attention. "He would not allow me to pick up the baby when he cried." "Every time I would give my attention to the baby he would demand that I do something for him." "He wanted all my attention, to be there when he wanted me. I just felt like a prisoner." Ann's husband left her and returned to his mother's home.

In such a marriage the mother will be experiencing great emotional upheaval struggling to do what is expected of her. She may be unable to meet these expectations because of her inability to give love and security to her infant. An unplanned pregnancy may be an interference in the life plan of a woman who is involved in other activities and does not particularly want the responsibility of rearing a child. These mothers all need assistance in verbalizing their thoughts and feelings to someone they can trust. They express feelings of anxiety, "How will I manage?" "I just can't do it." or some similar statement will give a clue to her frustration with her new role. Her anger spews forth as she projects blame either on her husband or herself. Then she feels guilty because she should be accepting her situation with happiness.

The religious person is very careful not to judge the mother. It is his training to expect that every woman wants to be a mother. It has been known to happen that a pastoral person has made the woman feel extremely guilty because of her inability to accept motherhood. Religious counselors need to know that by allowing the mother to explore her feelings in a non-judgmental atmosphere he will help her to gain insight and subsequent growth will occur. By helping the mother verbalize her problems and by reflecting back to her the thoughts expressed, reality will open up to her. This in turn will enable her to choose adequate coping mechanisms. Respecting her as a person, the minister allows her to be herself without rejection. She learns that she is a valued worthwhile individual.

The unplanned pregnancy may occur when the young couple wants to space their children or meet some major financial obligation. They both may be in school or working toward other goals. The pregnancy may be viewed as a shock at first. With assistance from the pastoral counselor, they are able to accept the new member joyfully. Reva Rubin describes the response of women who become pregnant unexpectedly. "A woman experiences pregnancy as a conditional state, approached questioningly, even searchingly, with periods of exploration and trials during which she accepts some answers as satisfying and as of 'good fit' and rejects others, a state characterized by a tendency to be more aware of time and of who and what kind of person she really is."[8] The couple need to reassess their goals and with the counselor's support are able to view the situation realistically.

A middle-aged couple may respond similarly if they have tried unsuccessfully to have children earlier in their marriage. They may feel pregnancy to be an intrusion into their lives. Usually, after children are reared and gone from the home couples begin to enjoy their middle years; both are more mature and experienced. They will feel shock and surprise. If they are mature they will discuss their feelings openly and work together to face the problem. Some couples welcome the assistance of their minister because they know he will encourage them in their decision.

The mother who has established a life for herself outside of her home will experience mixed emotions of anger and guilt. She may even consider an abortion as her only solution but there is guilt because of her moral values concerning life. She may feel anger toward herself for being so careless. She may blame her husband for reasons not too clear in her own mind. Allowing her to express her feelings openly and accepting how she feels gives her reassurance that she is not alone. She needs to know that she can have these kinds of feelings and someone understands and is ready to help her without rejection.

The effective pastoral person is exceptionally kind, understanding and unbiased when counseling pregnant women with these specific attitudes. Some religious counselors have biased opinions concerning women who feel rebellious toward pregnancy. They often judge these women from the male orientation and assume that they are selfish if they do not enjoy pregnancy or children. A woman in such a dilemma is suffering intensely already and doesn't need to hear that "God wills it" or "God will take care of it." She needs a person who can comfort her by accepting her as she is by allowing her to express her feelings without rejection. Gradually as she begins to gain insight into herself, she can be guided to explore her feelings in depth. She can grow and accept her life situation. The minister readily experiences the uniqueness of each human person because he is open to their suffering.

Every human experiences his life situation in a different way. They do not fit into a category nor can they be measured according to a particular criterion. The spiritual leader involved with parents experiencing difficulties due to an unexpected pregnancy, be it a middle age pregnancy, health of the mother, fear of some deformity or because of finances, views each as a unique situation. Listening to their difficulties and helping them to explore alternate ways of coping allows for growth as they accept their life situation. The adaptational process develops over a period of time and the support from the minister in a therapeutic relationship will encourage the couple to find meaning in their life.

Parents of a Defective Child

Parents of a deformed or defective infant may need to talk

about their disappointment with someone who can help them. They usually call for their minister. They experience a loss as their anticipatory fantasies have not materialized. They are victims of many conflicting feelings. The mother feels anger and resentment, blaming her husband or her doctor. It is very difficult for her to see her baby. Some women reject the baby by refusing to believe that it is theirs. The question arises out of guilt, "What have I done that caused this?" or "God must be punishing me." "Why me?" She can tell you about some insignificant "sin" from her early life. If it is her first child, she questions her femininity or her ability to have normal children. She feels depressed and anxious about her ability to care for the child. The father of the child also may question his masculinity. Was he responsible for some genetic defect and will it happen again? The husband may blame his wife and make her feel more inadequate and guilty. This feeling is very difficult to work through realistically.

The pastoral leader works very closely with the health team so the parents can experience support from all those involved in their welfare. The minister is supportive to the parents when the physician plans surgical intervention to correct the defect or when they need to make a decision concerning institutional care versus home care. Therapeutic intervention is essential for these parents as they try to find meaning in their sufferings. Most parents are willing to do everything they can to give their child love and security; they just need someone to help them feel comfortable in their decision.

When malfunctions occur in a first child the question arises, "Will we be able to have a 'normal' child?" Genetic counseling should be encouraged for these parents. The minister working closely with the physician and nurses reinforces their suggestions and recommendations. Many couples do not always hear everything at first. Blocking may occur because of the high anxiety level they are experiencing. They have many questions that a religious leader could help to answer. He should encourage them in their search to find acceptable attitudes that will assist them in facing and coping with their situation.

Parents who have a growing love and deep respect for each

other will be able to move toward acceptance more readily than a couple involved in a poor relationship. It has been known that a husband was so shattered by the experience that he blamed his wife and filed suit for divorce. It took months in therapy to help the young mother to adjust to her situation. She had to regain confidence in herself as a woman. Having a deformed or defective child is a very traumatic experience for parents as there is concern in caring adequately for the child. A religious counselor can give the necessary reassurance as they begin to adjust to the needs of their child. The physician usually explains to parents the many physiological causes of deformity-defects giving them scientific facts; telling them of areas that are being researched. A well informed minister knows some basic genetics so he can reinforce the physician's explanations. Physicians do explain known or probable causes to parents and encourage seeking genetic counseling. The health team at this time needs to work together to help the parents cope. As Owens states, "We should expect these parents to show signs of grief. They have to come to terms with a very painful situation, largely unexpected, often with a poor prognosis for the child. If their child is alive, but may die, they will try one way or another to relieve feelings of pain and anxiety but, at the same time, they may find it extremely difficult to do something about the situation for their child."[9]

A woman who has a "miscarriage," a stillbirth or a child who dies shortly after birth experiences a loss and needs to grieve. Allowing her to talk about her feelings is necessary as she needs someone to listen to her and understand her grief. She needs to express her feelings of anger and hurt. She has guilt feelings and often asks "Why me?" "What have I done to deserve this?" or "God is punishing me." A hospital chaplain or the minister is an appropriate person to help the mother work through her feelings, especially when burial arrangements are made.

This is an opportune time to help parents view God as a loving person, who cares and does not punish. The concept of suffering as part of human living is valuable, since we mature as persons and grow in love when we learn to accept our suffering. The patient and her husband are suffering and experiencing loss. They need support. They need to feel someone cares and understands their loss as a unique loss. Joan Marie Johnson describes her own experience, and states, that "parents may wonder if the death is punishment for past wrong doings or perhaps, because the child was not wanted. Regardless of these feelings, it is important that parents be discouraged from trying to place blame. They need reassurance that past misdeeds or thoughts had nothing to do with the baby's death." She continues by saying, "giving false reassurance is also dangerous, for even though the chances are that another pregnancy will result in a normal infant, there are no guarantees. Reminding the mother that she has other children is not helpful, for there is little difference between losing a child before birth or at any age, the void cannot be filled with another child."[10] This mother has summarized how important we are to each other and in time of need the comfort of someone who understands the pain. A person grieving needs to feel the presence of caring people and not be left alone. Aloneness can be agonizing.

Parents coping with a premature delivery benefit from the support of the pastoral person as they work through their feelings of inadequacy and doubt. They are experiencing disappointment because their expectations for a mature "healthy" baby did not materialize. They question themselves as to the cause and feel guilty. They experience a threatened loss if the infant is in the intensive nursery fighting for his life. They need support in their suffering and to cope adequately until the infant is out of danger. If the infant dies after a long period of time they will experience grief and need to work through their own grief separately. The religious leader is perceptive of their feelings and helps them grow from the experience preventing any maladaption. Usually the premature infant will remain in the hospital after the mother has gone home delaying the acquaintance period between infant and mother. This is a difficult time for a mother as she is generally not involved in the actual care of her infant, feeling inadequate and an outsider. Some hospitals recognize the importance of the mother and involve her in the care of her infant but some do not; it is then she needs an understanding person to hear her concerns and feelings.

The Unwed Mother

The unwed mother, particularly if she is an adolescent, needs understanding and acceptance in making her decisions. She may consider abortion, carrying the baby to term, keeping the infant, or giving it up for adoption. Establishing an environment that facilitates acceptance without threat of judgment is most conducive to encourage the person to be open. Adolescence is a time of crises. They are searching for their identity. Body changes occur, menses begins and secondary sex characteristics emerge. Their concerns are of body; how they look to others and how they see themselves. They experience some emotional instability, they become sensitive to others' opinions, responding angrily at times or very loving. They are maturing psychologically moving toward young adulthood. The process of maturity can be difficult if the young female does not experience an accepting relationship with her parents. Normal adjustment is disrupted when the family life is chaotic, and unrealistic or excessive demands are made upon the developing adult. When poor parental relationships exist the adolescent feels alone, unable to confirm her values or to sort out some of her beliefs. Feeling alone, anger may have its expression in rebellious behavior that may express defiance for parents and authority figures. Getting pregnant may be one way of expressing anger or rebellion. The reasons for the adolescent girl becoming pregnant are numerous. Some follow peer pressure to engage in sexual activity. Many young adolescent females engage in discussing their sexual activities making others feel that something is wrong with them if they don't. They then become involved sexually to be like the others. Unfortunately, some of these girls know very little about their bodies, and reproduction. Many do not have correct knowledge of contraception, so when they become sexually involved pregnancy may occur. This particular girl will be fearful and anxious with deep feelings of guilt. She feels confused and desperate since she had not prepared for this event. She needs someone to talk with who will be objective yet care enough about her to help her make decisions.

If she cannot talk with her mother or father she will go to her minister. She needs help in sorting out her feelings. She may express deep shame, guilt and fear. She needs a person to understand and help her gain insight into the reason she became pregnant. It could be to prove to her mother she is no longer a child. Or because of parental negativeness, she may feel she can never accomplish anything and by having a child, she is trying to prove her worth. A young woman may want to have a baby to love, because she feels her parents have never loved her. Her rationale is based on the belief that babies are lovable and love their mothers. It is extremely difficult to convey to the adolescent the responsibility involved in childrearing. Their fantasy does not include the fact that the growing infant has needs to be met twenty-four hours a day. She may express love for the father of the child and meet with parental disapproval and become pregnant to punish the parents for their strong possessiveness. She may get pregnant to force the father of the child into marriage. If this does not materialize the young woman may become depressed and possibly suicidal. She will need assistance in viewing her situation realistically and making some decisions.

The first decision that should be reached is to discuss her situation with her parents. They all need to express feelings. The minister can help them clarify these feelings so that problems can be solved in such a way that everyone will grow. Meeting with the family for a series of sessions will be necessary if she chooses to remain at home. There are homes where girls can go to await their babies if the young mother wants to keep her pregnancy secretive or not burden her parents.

The young mother should be encouraged to discuss her pregnancy and plans for the baby with the father if this is at all possible. It may be that the parents reject the father and feel he has no place in the problem. Yet, the unwed father has a responsibility to his unborn child; to give support to the mother if she decides to keep the child and raise it by herself. Pannor recommends that to help unwed fathers act responsibly, "they can be encouraged to stand by the unmarried mother, which is of extreme importance to her and help prevent feelings that she alone carried the burden and shows that both parties involved are sharing responsibilities."[11] If she decides to give the child up for adoption both can begin anew, hopefully as more responsible persons.

Some unwed adolescent girls become pregnant fulfilling their mother's wish to have a baby. Their mothers for some reason can no longer bear children but want to have a child around the home to love or feel needed. They will encourage their daughters to become sexually active hoping they become pregnant. The mother will be oversolicitous and anxious to have her daughter with her child at home so she can feel like a mother again. The young mother needs assistance to explore her feelings as she may feel the entrapment.

There are agencies in the community that can assist the unwed mother during her pregnancy and help her to plan for the future. With proper counseling she can accept her situation realistically and become more knowledgeable. These adolescents should be encouraged to become involved in prenatal classes. It is one way of assisting them to become responsible persons. They need to have a clear understanding about sex, their sexual feelings in relation to themselves as persons. Adolescence is a difficult time and they need adults with whom they can openly discuss their beliefs without reproach. They need to test out their opinions with others to learn how to evaluate themselves. Gradually they learn to accept their place in society as adults. They become responsible for their own actions, are aware of how these actions affect others and acquire the ability to grow from experiences.

Gynecological Patients

The removal of the uterus, ovaries and/or tubes for some medical reason can be a traumatic experience for some women. They have fears and anxieties concerning their ability to function as a woman. They express loss; loss of function comparable to loss of body image. "That which makes me a woman no longer exists." Some women may feel relieved. Aside from experiencing the post-surgical state a particular woman will grieve deeply if her uterus was taken out possibly for cancer. She mourns the loss of her "womanhood" or as so many have expressed "my femininity," or "I can't have any more children." This seems to be of equal concern with the fear of the cancer metastatisizing. The physician can lessen anxiety by explaining what he actually did and why he may have done a total hysterectomy. Most physicians are open with their patients and usually explain the physical status. The nurse becomes aware of the patient who is feeling depressed and somewhat irritable or she may find her crying.

The religious counselor complements the nurse's support by giving the patient the opportunity to view her feelings realistically and develop a deeper insight into herself as a human person who is a female. She is encouraged to view her relationship with her husband and her role as a mother with a positive attitude. She will experience some depression as the result of the surgery and the body part loss. Listening empathetically conveys to the person understanding and genuine concern. Reflecting her feelings and thoughts back to her will help her to gain insight into her own behavior. She will then find alternate ways of coping satisfactorily with her life situation. The religious counselor is the person who can help those who are searching for meaning in a life situation, especially at a time when one is experiencing aloneness.

In conclusion, an effective pastoral person who is involved in helping women and their families meet these kinds of problems is mature and aware of himself as a person. In being involved in the lives of people he grows more as a person. From the enrichment of the many lives he touches and those who touch his, he becomes wiser and more compassionate. A pastoral person cannot be involved therapeutically with those who seek his services without becoming a better person himself.

NOTES

1. Erich Fromm, *The Art of Loving* (New York: Bantam Books, 1963), p. 50.

2. Joyce Travelbee, R.N., M.S.N., *Interpersonal Aspects of Nursing* (Philadelphia: F.A. Davis Company, 1971), p. 136.

3. Ashley Montagu, *Touching* (New York: Harper & Row, Perennial Library, 1972), pp. 77-78.

4. Virginia Satir, *Conjoint Family Therapy* (Palo Alto, Cal.: Science and Behavior Books, Inc., 1967), p. 11.

5. John J. Evoy, S.J., and Sister Maureen O'Keefe, S.S.N.D., *The Man and the Woman* (New York: Sheed and Ward, 1968), p. 107.

6. Harry Stack Sullivan, *The Interpersonal Theory of Psychiatry* (New York: W.W. Norton & Company, Inc., 1953), p. 74.

7. Adrian Van Kaam, *The Art of Existential Counseling* (Wilkes-Barre, Pa.: Dimension Books, 1966), p. 31.

8. Reva Rubin, R.N., M.S., "Cognitive Style in Pregnancy," *The American Journal of Nursing*, March 1970, p. 503.

9. Charlotte Owens, "Parents' Reactions to Defective Babies," *Maternal Health Nursing* (Dubuque, Iowa: Wm. C. Brown Company Publishers, 1967), p. 199.

10. Joan Marie Johnson, "Stillbirth—A Personal Experience," *American Journal of Nursing*, September 1972, pp. 1595-1596.

11. Reuben Pannor, "The Forgotten Man," *Nursing Outlook*, November 1970, pp. 36-37.

SELECTED BIBLIOGRAPHY

Bell and Vogel, "The Emotionally Disturbed Child as a Family Scapegoat," *A Modern Introduction To The Family* (New York: Free Press, 1963), pp. 382-397.

Bell, Robert R. (ed.), *Studies in Marriage and the Family* (New York: Thomas Y. Crowell Company, 1968).

Bergerson, B., *et. al.*, *Current Concepts in Clinical Nursing* (St. Louis: Mosby Company, 1967).

Bruce, S., "Reactions of Nurses and Mothers to Stillbirths," *Nursing Outlook* 10:88-91, 1962.

Caplan, Gerald, "Patterns of Parental Response to the Crisis of Premature Birth: A Preliminary Approach to Modifying the Mental Health Outcome," *Psychiatry* 23:365-374, 1960.

Cavan, Ruth Schonle (ed.), *Marriage and Family in the Modern World—A Book of Readings* (New York: Thomas Y. Crowell Company, 1969).

Eshleman, J. (ed.), *Perspectives in Marriage and the Family* (Boston: Allyn and Bacon Inc., 1969), pp. 644-696.

Friedman, S., *et al.*, "Behavioural Observations of Parents Anticipating the Death of a Child," *Pediatrics*, 32:619, Oct. 1963.

Goldfogel, Linda, "Working with the Parents of a Dying Child," *American Journal of Nursing* 71:1675-1679, 1970.

Kallop, Fritzi, R.N., B.S., "Working With Parents Through a Devastating Experience: The Birth of a Mongoloid Child," *JOGN Nursing*, May/June 1973.

Kaplan, D. and E. Mason, "Maternal Reactions to Premature Birth Viewed as an Acute Emotional Disorder," *American Journal of Orthopsychiatry*, Vol. 30, No. 3, 1960.

Kelman, Howard R., "The Effect of a Brain-Damaged Child on the Family," *Brain Damage in Children—The Biological and Social Aspects*, edited by Herbert G. Birch (Baltimore: Williams and Wilkins Company, 1963), pp. 77-99.

Kennell, Rolnick, "Discussing Problems in Newborn Babies with Their Parents," *Pediatrics*, 1960.

Lee, Jane, "Emotional Reactions to Trauma," *Nursing Clinics of North America* 5:577-587, Dec. 1970.

Legeay *et al.*, "Impact of Mental Retardation on Family Life," *American Journal of Nursing* 66:1062-1065, May 1966.

LeMasters, E., *Parents in Modern America* (Homewood, Ill.: Dorsey Press, 1970).

Lukens, K. and C. Panter, *Thursday's Child Has Far To Go* (Englewood Cliffs, N.J.: Prentice-Hall, 1969).

Mathis, James L., M.D., "Psychologic Aspects of Surgery on Female Reproductive Organs," *JOGN Nursing*, Jan./Feb. 1973.

Owens, C., "Parents Reactions to Defective Babies," *American Journal of Nursing 64:83-86, 1964.*

Parad, Howard (ed.), *Crisis Intervention: Selected Readings* (New York: Family Service Association, 1965).

Rainwater, Lee, "Some Aspects of Lower Class Sexual Behavior," *Medical Aspects of Human Sexuality*, February 1968, pp. 15-25.

Reitz, Martha, "Habilitation: The Study of a Child with a Congenital Anomaly," *Nursing Clinics of North America*, Sept. 1966, pp. 451-457.

Solnit, A. and M. Stark, "Mourning and the Birth of a Defective Child," *Psychoanalytic Study of the Child*, 16:523-537, 1961.

Susser, M.W. and W. Watson, "Infant to Adult," pp. 241-290; "Mating and Marriage," pp. 202-240; and "The Cycle of Family Development," pp. 188-201, *Sociology in Medicine* (London: Oxford University Press, 1962).

Sussman, Marvin (ed.), *Sourcebook in Marriage and the Family*, 2nd edition (Boston: Houghton Mifflin Co., 1963).

Tisza, V., "Management of the Parents of the Chronically Ill Child," *American Journal of Orthopsychiatry*, 32:53-59, Jan. 1962.

5. Ministering to Persons Who Have Suffered Amputation or Disfigurement

When the adjustment to loss is discussed, generally it is considered only in terms of death, especially of a spouse, parent or child. In reality though, loss involves losing anyone who was close to you or losing any thing of great material or great emotional value. This can be a move involving a change of residence which means leaving valued friends and a secure known environment. It can be the loss of a lifetime accomplishment or loss of a home destroyed by fire or by natural disaster; the loss of a valued job for a person who has worked hard to achieve a successful, satisfying position. In this chapter, however, our discussion will be limited to the loss of a major part of the body, such as the amputation of a limb, removal of a breast, removal of a bodily organ, or some disfiguring injury. Any one of these losses causes a person to suffer a loss experience and threatens a person's body image and self-concept. Thus any major disruption in life such as one of these losses becomes a crisis in a person's life. Nancy Martin in her chapter, "Nursing in Rehabilitation" explains, "In permanent illness or disability the individual will physically never again be as he was premorbidly. Whatever physical changes occurred are irreversible. This person cannot be cured—he cannot be made whole. The lost function or part will not be restored. Although in some cases it is possible to substitute for the loss in such manner as to allow the person to lead, 'a normal life,' the disability remains. The obvious and permanent physical individual's concept of self."[1]

Developing a Body Image and Self-Concept

Body image begins early in life and extends from infancy through adulthood. At first the infant's world is diffuse—he is still one with his mother on whom he depends for everything. Ideally he is fondled, caressed and fed by mother and so feels his oneness with her. This is where a child first feels security and develops trust. Gradually, there becomes an awareness of separateness from his mother and interaction begins taking place between the child and his mother and other people. This interaction with the people in the child's world and the objects in his environment will make the initial impacts in his life of being acceptable or inferior. What he believes he is as a person, he learns from the expressions of attitudes toward him from the significant persons in his life, namely his parents and siblings. He develops a positive mental picture about himself if his relationships were pleasing. He then integrates his self concept and body image, and views himself as being a loved, valued and worthwhile person. Gradually he learns the give and take of life because he feels accepted as a person; a unique human being.

These early experiences in life are also important because they are the basis upon which subsequent experiences are interpreted. The child who experiences positive relationships early in life will trust others and have a view of the world around him as warm and friendly. He will then continue to develop his body image and self concept in a way that he knows he is lovable. Adolescence is a time when his body image begins to change. Along with the change of image comes the search for identity. He places great emphasis on his body and how he looks to others. He needs a great deal of reassurance from his parents who can help him to maintain a positive view of himself as a unique person. He then moves into adulthood as a mature individual capable of accepting himself as part of society. Stone and Church explain "that the mature individual has to be able to live comfortably with his own body, whether it be strong or weak, handsome or ugly, healthy or failing. This does not mean that he fails to groom it, or tend to its ills, but that he can be at ease about it, not wasting his time in futile laments or hypochondria."[2]

On the other hand, an adolescent who never feels his parents' acceptance, suffers a very traumatic experience. If he was made to feel inadequate in any way, his self concept will be low and he will view his body as inferior. He could suffer some distortions of his body image and may develop a distorted view of himself. He may develop an exaggerated interest in his body to strive toward acceptance. This can be done through clothing styles, developing strong muscular bodies and through hair styles. It can be seen in some of our men who place great priority on physical fitness. They drive to keep their "bodies in shape." It is also evident in the adolescent female who may go to extremes in maintaining perfect posture, clothing extravaganzas, or in withdrawal and hiding. Many females in our country have been reared to feel inferior to males and are taught that they must be physically beautiful to attract males. Our daily advertisements stress the female "perfect body."

When this individual is confronted with a disabling illness or a disfigurement, he or she suffers deeply and is often unable to cope with the change. Such a person mourns this loss without ever being able to accept it; withdraws, becomes depressed and will not become involved completely in rehabilitation. Schoenberg and Carr describe it as "the body image has integrity and intactness which are presumed to reflect basic aspects of one's ego integration. When this integration is weak, disruption of the body image through surgery or amputation may precipitate blatant psychotic or delusional behavior. Even in well adjusted persons, however, the almost universal reaction to such loss is that of grief, accompanied by depression and anxiety."[3]

Thus normally everyone who suffers a drastic change in life will grieve the loss but how he moves toward adaptation depends upon his ability to handle crisis. The change will cause an emotional crisis. He is no longer the same as he used to be. His body is now different. He must learn a new way to live and as he learns he mourns his loss, whether it is longing for the old body or the old way of life. His ability to cope depends upon how readily he expresses his feelings concerning his loss. Mourning is a lonely process which must be worked through alone. There may be many people helping, as the health team in rehabilitation, yet the patient feels isolated. He may say, "You can't possibly know how I feel, it is my body." How true! We can know how he feels only as he expresses his feelings and thoughts. When a pastoral counselor listens to a patient explain how desperate he feels about his inability to function as he did when he felt whole, the minister learns how painful the loss can be.

Different Types of Losses through Sickness or Injury

The impact of the shock or disbelief in individuals who experience the loss of a limb is felt when he sees his arm or leg missing. His ability to adjust will depend upon the view he has of himself as a person. If he has a positive concept of himself he will likely move toward adjustment to his new body image. He will grieve normally as he begins his rehabilitation. The person who is unable to cope with his loss will need assistance in verbalizing his feelings and thoughts. Accepting him without a leg or arm will be reassuring to the individual that he is still a person. Working with the health team, the minister reinforces the goals the rehabilitation group has set for the patient. The pastoral counselor is a source of encouragement to the person by listening to him and explaining to him any regime he does not understand. Counseling with the family is necessary so they can accept his loss and make the necessary adjustments to allow for the change. The family members will also need support as they cope with the change. Offering alternate views concerning the loss will be valuable especially if they are feeling anger or guilt. They need to express these feelings and the minister understanding the pain and frustration felt at this time is a source of strength to them. The patient and his family need assistance in order for them to accept the change and to develop a new and comfortable relationship because often the family roles are reversed or resumed in a different way. Sometimes, spouses are

unable to accept the change in their partners, resulting in abandonment and divorce. Clara divorced her husband several
months after he had a leg amputated to stop a cancerous
growth. She often remarked, "I can't bear to look at his
stump." "I can't accept all the burden of taking care of him; I
want to have a whole man to take care of me." She was unable
to accept the reality of the new change that demanded responsibility from her.

The person who suffers partial paralysis and asphasia due
to a stroke requires a great deal of psychological assistance to
promote successful rehabilitation and the patient's family
should be involved in the rehabilitation. Emphasis needs to be
placed on their response to his change. The patient had neurolo-
gical changes involving perception, visual and motor areas
which add to his suffering. He mourns the loss of his health and
the life he once lived. He feels deep frustration because of his
dependency on others for his needs, and because of his inability
to make himself understood. The religious counselor understands some of the feelings this patient is experiencing even
though he is unable to express himself clearly or adequately.
Speaking slowly, clearly and directly to the patient will enable
him to understand what is being communicated. Facilitating an
accepting environment without rejection allows the patient to
express himself the only way he knows, and shows respect for
him as a person. The minister has the opportunity to reinforce
the patient's efforts to rehabilitate himself and helps motivate
him to achieve the goals established by the health team. The
stroke victim feels anxious, angry, frustrated and guilty concerning his malady and mourns the loss of his ability to control
his life.

The rehabilitative process to be successful depends a great
deal upon the patient's response to his disabling illness. He
needs to be seen as a human person who is incapacitated, unable
to do things he was accustomed to doing. His security has been
disrupted and the possibility of death is frightening. Being physically disabled depresses the patient as it may place him into
the group who are considered "handicapped" and "crippled."
Patients may respond by saying, "Who wants a cripple; a noth-

ing?" He is telling you how low his self esteem is and of his inability to view himself as a person. The religious counselor listens intently and responds appropriately to the person who is lashing out in anger and guilt; unable to cope. Close collaborative relationships with the health team are necessary to understand the patient's progress. The pastoral visitor is aware of the goals of the group to rehabilitate the person. Attempting to understand the patient's view of himself in relation to his illness is the way the pastoral counselor learns how best to assist the person to cope adequately. He needs a great deal of emotional support and encouragement as he is trying to learn to walk again and to speak audibly.

The paraplegic or spinal cord injured mourns in a different way, possibly by using denial and by not getting involved in his rehabilitative program. He has his own unique difficulties to cope with; a total relearning to live with a body that no longer moves. He has physical limitations and learning to care for himself can be difficult unless those helping him know how he feels about himself. How does he view life? What meaning does it have for him now? Listening to the patient express himself will help him verbalize how he views his disability. Being alert to his non-verbal behavior can be an indicator to how he feels, especially when he appears involved in his rehabilitative program, yet resists and withdraws from sound activities. The entire team plan and work together to continually evaluate how the patient is progressing toward adapting to his new life. It will be painful and he may resist by refusing care or not showing up for some important activity, such as his physical therapy. He may express some of his anger through various hostile behavior; throwing objects, using abusive language, or withdrawing and refusing to talk. Tom, a 30 year old paraplegic, would display his anger by throwing things at the nursing personnel and screaming at them, "Leave me alone—I don't want to be bothered. I don't want anyone doing anything for me." He spent a great deal of his time sleeping and refusing to get involved in his rehabilitative program. Throughout this ordeal the sick person benefits from understanding and from being made aware that he is accepted as an individual, a unique human person despite the fact he is disabled. He is well aware that he can no longer have his old body that gave him a freedom he no longer possesses. He may regress, becoming very depressed, possibly suicidal. At this time he needs a "someone" to do crisis intervention. Accepting him and encouraging him to express his feelings will help him to develop a realistic perception of his situation.

Emphasis needs to be placed on the positive attributes he possesses; that being a person means growing from his sufferings. The minister can be very supportive and reassuring to him as he struggles to accept the raw reality of his disability. The family must be involved in his rehabilitation program as many changes may have to be made and dealt with realistically. If roles are to be reversed assistance may be necessary to adjust from former established roles. The family system is now altered and relationships need strengthening for them to cope adequately as they gradually adapt to a new way of living. The pastoral counselor, working with the health team, knows what areas to reinforce as the family adjusts to the patient and the patient to his family.

When a young man suffers the loss of his sexual function in a disabling injury or illness, it is very important for the minister to explore how he perceives his body and what value he places on it. The young male has a very difficult time adjusting to this loss if he learned from his parents that maleness involves having a strong muscular body and that physical strength and attractiveness are mandatory to be successful and acceptable. The sexual image of this young man is integrated in the concept of maleness which has developed during his entire lifetime. His attitudes toward his sexuality are the result of his environment. Such a young man probably is more concerned with his ability to have an erection and to function adequately in the area of sex than in becoming involved in a meaningful relationship. The pastoral counselor ministering to such a young man assists him to verbalize his concerns and to understand how these attitudes learned as a child affect his progress. This area, which must be explored with any patient who has suffered a disruption in his body image, is doubly important for this young man who has lost his sexual function. If the religious counselor has some difficulty discussing this area with the patient, he needs to examine his own attitudes and views. The advantage of working as a team with other health workers is to exchange findings and seek ways to assist the patient to move toward growth with his new body.

This concept of sexuality is also applied to females, as they learn their sexual roles from their mothers in their developing years. Many learn that sex is dirty, shameful and something to be tolerated, leaving many women with the concept that sex is not to be enjoyed; they may view themselves as inferior beings. The pastoral counselor ministering to a female patient who is experiencing the loss of a sexual organ such as uterus, ovaries or breast examines his own attitude toward women. He is a tremendous help to them if instead of reinforcing their poor concept of femininity, he offers them acceptance and understanding, indicating that all of us, men and women, are human persons, who have complementary roles, equally important. Not only does the wife need ministering when she has suffered the loss of some reproductive organ, but so does the husband. The wife, for example, who lost her breast due to a malignancy will be concerned about the cancer metatasizing, the ugly scar, and her femininity. When she feels acceptance from her husband and those involved in her care, she can readily adapt to her new self image. The woman, however, who views her body as a sexual object to attract and seduce males as the basis of her femininity will experience the disfigurement profoundly. She may withdraw, becoming progressively depressed and if her husband rejects her because of his inability to accept the change, she will feel totally rejected. She will make statements such as, "I can't stand it. I'm so ugly." "How horrible it is to have lost my breast." "Who can love half a woman?" These are all giving clues to her inner feelings concerning herself as a woman. Establishing a warm accepting relationship with the patient is important as it allows her to feel her worth. Encouraging the patient to verbalize her thoughts and feelings will take time and gentle persuasion can be used to help her view herself as a person. Emphasis on her unique attributes is a very real way of making her see herself as valued. Ministers having a genuine concern for people convey this through their non-verbal behavior and patients respond readily.

The psychosocial needs of a colostomy patient are to learn to live with a colostomy altered body and a life socially acceptable for them. They will need assistance to adjust to the change and develop an acceptable altered self concept. The preoperative interview with the physician is important. It is important for the patient to hear directly from the surgeon the reasons for the colostomy or osteomy. The other members of the health team prepare the patient for the change, each discipline offering support from their unique frame of reference. The minister reaffirms much of what the physician and nurses have offered in preparation and adds to it the spiritual aspect. He needs to have answers for, "Why me?" "Why do I have to have this done?" The patient's response to his surgery depends upon his early childhood experiences in the development of his body concept. During the toilet training period a child learns to view his bodily excrement either as something pleasing and pleasurable or as dirty and inferior. This is learned from his early relationship with his mother who transmits to him warmth and acceptance or she may have instilled into him that his feces are dirty, making him feel ashamed. Having to deal with his excrement causes great repulsion and makes him view himself as inferior. This remains throughout the person's life and causes a great deal of emotional suffering when a colostomy is inevitable. Joseph a 60 year old laborer with a recent colostomy verbalized a great deal when he was learning to irrigate his colostomy. "How can I go anywhere among people with this to care for; it takes so long?" "What can I do about the terrible odor?" "I won't be able to go back to my old job and what do I do if my bag leaks?" He gradually learned to care for himself but he was always concerned about the odor and the possibility of his bag leaking. The osteomy clubs do a great deal for patients faced with permanent osteomas as their goal is to assist others like themselves to live a healthy acceptable life. The religious counselor involved in the rehabilitation of persons with osteomas is a contact with the local chapter and co-operates with their approach.

Conclusion

During the rehabilitation of a person who is experiencing a loss due to a permanent disability or illness he suffers acutely. The impact of the reality of his disruption can cause severe emotional upheavals and the health team uses all their skills to give the best care possible. Their goal is to assist those who experience an abrupt life change to resolve the immediate crisis so that, hopefully, rehabilitation will be successful. This is a difficult task as every human being has his own unique personality traits and ways of coping with life. Each person mourns his loss differently.

Since those involved in his care view him as an individual, they allow the sick person the freedom to choose to grow or to remain in his known secure world unable to grow. Thus, some, able with assistance to adjust, live a worthwhile life, while others unable to cope, develop maladaptions. Viktor Frankl says: "The freedom of a finite being such as man is a freedom within limits. Man is not free from conditions, be they biological or psychological or sociological in nature. But he is, and always remains, free to take a stand toward these conditions; he always retains the freedom to choose his attitude toward them. Man is free to rise above the plan of somatic and psychic determinants of his existence."[4] Man as a unique being can choose to work through his feelings or he can refuse and give in because the loss is too great to bear. A patient suffering drastic body changes has much to cope with and needs to know that many are ready to help him.

Being human involves suffering and man sees suffering as an intrusion into his life; therefore he responds. Suffering cannot be avoided and the ability to grow from it will be the meaning suffering has for each person. Frankl says: "Whenever one is confronted with an inescapable, unavoidable situation; whenever one has to face a fate which cannot be changed, e.g., an incurable disease, such as an inoperable cancer; just then one is given a last change to actualize the highest value, to fulfill the deepest meaning, the meaning of suffering."[5]

Ministers have a special contribution to make in the life of a person suffering, that of spiritual comfort. The therapeutic use of self is being sensitive to the person's spiritual needs and intervening to meet those needs to promote the growth of the person who must develop areas within himself to compensate for his inability to function as he did previously. The pastor counselor develops his own frame of reference concerning the development of body image in order to understand the response the patient expresses when his body image is distorted. Schoenberg and Carr describe an "individual's body image as being dependent on his ability to perceive his body and its parts realistically and to adapt to them as they actually exist. The ability to assess one's body and its parts is in turn related to early life experiences, especially the relationship with parents and other family members."[6]

Being involved in the rehabilitation of a patient with a loss of body image requires the religious counselor to give spiritual strength through the agonizing periods experienced in the struggle to accept disability. The minister overflowing with love for God, and those who are made in the image and likeness of God, imparts spiritual comfort, imitating God's love for each human person. Man is an embodied being, subject to pain, suffering, illness and death. It can be very depressing, struggling to live an altered life without love. To share again Frankl's thought which is most appropriate, he says: "Love is the only way to grasp another human being in the innermost core of his personality. No one can become fully aware of the very essence of another human being unless he loves him."[7]

The goal of the religious counselor is to love and give love to those who are suffering intensely from some disabling illness or injury that has caused an abrupt change in their life; that is giving love to those who see themselves as ugly and repulsive and to those who cannot accept themselves as persons because they have never experienced love. The religious who loves will touch the lives of those he becomes involved with and both will grow from the experiencing of loving.

NOTES

1. Nancy Martin, "Nursing in Rehabilitation," *Clinical Nursing*, edited by Irene Beland (New York: The Macmillan Company, 1970), p. 815.

2. L. Joseph Stone and Joseph Church, *Childhood and Adolescence* (New York: Random House, 1965), p. 340.

3. Bernard Schoenberg and Arthur C. Carr, "Loss of External Organs: Limb Amputation, Mastectomy and Disfiguration," *Loss and Grief: Psychological Management in Medical Practice* (New York: Columbia University Press, 1970), p. 121.

4. Viktor E. Frankl, *Psychotherapy and Existentialism* (New York: Simon and Schuster, 1967), p. 3.

5. Frankl, Viktor E., *Man's Search For Meaning* (Boston: Beacon Press, 1969), p. 114.

6. Schoenberg and Carr, *op. cit.*, p. 127.

7. Frankl, *op. cit.*, p. 113.

SELECTED BIBLIOGRAPHY

Anstice, E., "Coping after a Mastectomy," *Nursing Times* 66:882-883, July 9, 1970.

———, "The Emotional Operation," *Nursing Times*, 66:337-338, July 2, 1970.

Carty, E.A., "My, You're Getting Big," *Canadian Nurse* 66:40-43, August 1970.

Corbeil M., "Nursing Process for a Patient with a Body Image Disturbance," *Nursing Clinics of North America* 6:155-63, March 1971.

Davis, V., "Through the Bars of a Crib," *American Journal of Nursing* 71:1752-1753, Sept. 1971.

Fast, Julius, *Body Language* (New York: M. Evans & Co., Inc., 1971).

Felstein, I., "Psychological Problems and Synthetic Solutions," *Midwife Health Visit* 7:182-184, May 1971.

Fisher, Seymour and Sidney Cleveland, *Body Image and Personality* (Gloucester, Mass.: Peter Smith, 1968).

Jacobson, Linbania, "Illness and Human Sexuality," *Nursing Outlook*, Jan. 1974.

Kneisl, C.R., "Body Image—Its Meaning to the Self," *Journal of the New York Nurses Association* 2:29-35, Spring 1971.

Lee, J.M., "Emotional Reactions to Trauma," *Nursing Clinics of North America* 5:577-587, Dec. 1970.

Parsons, M.C., *et al.*, "Difficult Patients Do Exist," *Nursing Clinics of North America* 6:173-187, March 1971.

Rubin, Reva, "Body Image and Self Esteem," *Nursing Outlook*, June 1968.

Severyn, B.R., "Medical-Surgical Nursing. Nursing Implications With A Loss of Body Function," *ANA Reg. Clin. Conf.*, 233-41, 1969.

Shetlen, A., *Body Language and Social Order* (Englewood Cliffs, N.J.: Prentice-Hall, 1972).

Torrie, A., "Mastectomy—The Emotional Operation," *Nursing Mirror* 132:34-35, May 28, 1971.

Waldrop, Rosemarie and Nelson Howe, *Body Image* (New York: Wittenborn, 1970).

6. Ministering to Patients in Critical Care Units

The hospital has within it specialized units to care for people with various kinds of sicknesses. When a person is suffering from an illness or injury that is "presently life threatening," he is often treated in the intensive care or cardiac care unit which is staffed by physicians, nurses, and medical technicians who are experts in treating and caring for the critically or seriously ill person. The professionals working in these specialized units are skilled, knowledgeable individuals who are continually assessing the ill person's needs in an effort to reverse the crises situations by using highly complex machinery, such as monitors, defibrillators, hypothermia units, respiratory and suction apparatuses.

The personnel are hovering over the patient continuously providing life-saving measures. He may be immobilized on a bed with respiratory devices forcing and pumping air into his lungs. Both his arms may have intravenous solutions or blood going simultaneously. A monitor may be beeping constantly and tubes may be coming out of various parts of his body. Superimposed on his physiological stress is the stress caused by the sensory overload from the intensive care environment. Listening to constant hissing of oxygen and beeps of monitors alone can cause anxiety. He can't turn them off nor can he walk away from them. In addition, the personnel check his vital signs regularly causing an interruption in his sleep. Some patients may be unable to communicate at all if oxygen is being given by mask or a tracheotomy. This is often true of patients who have survived a major accident or have had some dramatic type of surgery. No wonder then that these patients experience mental confusion, misperceptions, and become disoriented. Some have been known to become extremely agitated and restless, to pull out the tubes or sometimes to become violent. The patient struggling to maintain life may move in and out of a conscious state or he may be so confined that the sensory stimuli are limited. He may be unable to react or interact with his immediate environment. This causes sensual and perceptual distortions. The interruption of the biorhythms and circadian rhythms of the person can cause distortions very similar to psychotic-life state.

Thus the environment of the critical care unit presents a strange unknown world for the patient and his family. The emotional impact for the patient from the shock state is profound as he experiences deep stress. His usual coping mechanism is no longer adequate as he struggles to keep himself together. This makes him feel helpless and fearful. He is losing control and needs to depend on those around him to meet his most basic needs for survival. His self image has also been shattered.

The staff are sensitive to the patient's physical and psychosocial needs. They try to understand the patient's response to the critical care unit and are aware of the teaching of Janet Smith who states: "The necessity of employing highly technical and precise measures to preserve life in a crisis situation commonly found in critical care units can create an environment totally alien and threatening to the patient. The complicated equipment necessary for maintenance of life requires unquestionable expertise on the part of personnel involved in the care of these patients."[1]

The staff attempt to reduce the patient's anxiety and confusion by acquainting him with his environment, explaining the reasons for his specific kind of treatment, orienting him to time, day and, if possible, having something in his cubicle that is a familiar object. Some patients like their family pictures or their own clock in a place where they can see it. The personnel make every effort to maintain an environment that will reduce the stimuli overload and minimize sensory deprivation. They are a group of professionals who work very closely with each other collaboratively in order to give the patient the best care possible. Assisting patients to cope with serious illness requires those

involved in his care continually to assess his progress and needs.
Once the patient's immediate physiological needs are met adequately, efforts are made to lessen his anxiety by meeting his
needs for security and belonging and reinforcing his sense of
worth.

Emotions of the Patient

The patient's immediate response, then, to an abrupt
change in life style by a life threatening illness or injury is
tinged with confusion and anxiety. His anxiety is intense not
only because of the new surroundings but more importantly
because of his fear of dying and non-being. The patient thinks
to himself, "I must be dying. Why else would I be getting all
this attention? I never saw any healthy patient being cared for
by so many people at the same time."

The coronary patient may exhibit anxiety in a very calm
manner, signaling denial of the illness. He is unable to cope
with the stress in any way except to block out the reality that he
is suffering a heart attack. If the patient admitted to himself the
seriousness of his condition, he would then have to face the possibility of death. Since that thought is too frightening, the patient uses the defense mechanism of denial. Physicians and
nurses are aware of this response among coronary patients as it
is unusual for patients to complain of being upset or even to appear apprehensive. They observe the physical symptoms of anxiety such as restlessness, rapid pulse, increased respirations, increased blood pressure, and excessive perspiration in a person
who appears calm and self-controlled. Some patients, though,
may express their anxieties and fears and these are usually
about the seriousness of their illness. How will he adjust to a
different way of life, his family, his job, and most of all, the
possibility of an early death? Thus, anxiety is normal among
coronary patients and it is manifested in some way in their behavior. However, this varies with each individual. Mr. Bernard,
a 32 year old coronary patient, verbalized his concern, "How

can I ever work again to support my family?" "I still get weak easily with the slightest exertion and I don't sleep too well." The mental mechanisms used by each individual will be different as he will use the method of coping that was used previously in any other crisis experienced in his life.

This response is similar to the feelings experienced by a patient anticipating major surgery, (for example, a patient facing open-heart surgery). The individual's fear of surgery is based on what he believes that surgery will do to him. The loss of a body part causes fear concerning the ability to cope with it afterward. A person faced with radical throat surgery will have deep fears about the possibility of suffocating to death or how he will adjust to his inability to communicate verbally. The person faced with brain surgery will have deep fears of never being what he used to be. The possibly of paralysis could leave him an invalid. The loss of a limb by amputation or any mutilating surgery will cause anxiety and mental suffering.

Helplessness is perhaps the strongest emotion the person in a critical unit feels. Before this hospitalization he was probably very active, working forty hours a week and bringing home a paycheck. He probably controlled his life, deciding where he would go and when. He might even have been a foreman at a factory or an executive of some company, and many people were dependent upon him. Now, as a very sick person, he has lost his freedom. He can't go whenever he wants to and possibly can't even change his position in bed without assistance. His role in life has changed radically from a state of complete independence to complete dependence. This threatens his self-image and causes him to question his value as a human being.

Another feeling the sick person experiences is isolation. All of his familiar surroundings have abruptly disappeared. He is not lying in his own comfortable bed; he is surrounded by strangers; the familiar trinkets in his home have been replaced by monitors and other highly complex machinery; he only sees his wife and loved ones for a short time each day; he knows there are other patients around him, but usually he can't see them and doesn't know how sick they are. Thus the patient in the critical care unit has been literally cut off from his familiar world and often ushered suddenly into a completely new world. Is it any wonder that he feels isolated and fearful?

Once the acute situation is over and the patient is faced with a long convalescence, he will experience different emotions as he begins to move toward adjustment. The reality of his condition has made its impact and will be expressed by anger and guilt. Busch and Gallo describe "the overt anger as possibly being directed towards the staff, he demands and whines. The displacement of anger on others helps to slow down the impact and the expression of anger itself gives the patient a sense of power in a seemingly helpless state."[2] His anger turned inward causes depression and he will ask, "Why me? Why at this particular time?" If he is a young executive he feels deprived of life and cheated. He may blame others for his misfortune. He pities himself, thinking he will be an invalid all his life and this too effects his self-image. This type of patient needs to express anger and guilt without feeling less a person.

Gradually the patient begins to face his life realistically as he adapts to his new self-image. He begins to make real efforts toward his own rehabilitation and he needs the support of his family. He is very much aware of the response of those involved in his care. His acceptance by the significant people in his life gives him new hope that he is acceptable. Being acceptable elevates his self-image. He feels that he is a worthy, valued human person.

Ministering to the Seriously Ill Patient

The minister who visits the critical care units regularly develops a good working relationship with the staff. This makes for open communications between the minister and staff who are working collaboratively in behalf of the patient. Most nurses and physicians readily share with him their observations regarding patients. Then he is of vital help to the patient who is struggling to adapt to the environment and his serious condition. Understanding how the person is progressing and responding to serious illness must be known before attempting to intervene. Working as part of the health team, a pastoral person helps the patient through his helplessness and need for control by reinforcing positively what is being done for him. The minister is the person whom the patient sees daily as someone who has time to spend with him. This lessens his sense of isolation and loneliness. Visiting the seriously ill person frequently with a definite purpose will lessen the great anxiety that he experiences. His sense of security and belonging is strengthened when the patient feels someone is there who understands him. When a patient is obviously very apprehensive about being in the critical care unit, the pastoral person might say, "You are fearful about being in here. Could you tell me what frightens you most?" Or he might say, "You must be having difficulty adjusting to this ward since you have been so active until recently and accustomed to being the bread-winner of the family." Statements like this assure the patient that the pastoral visitor is with him, that he is not alone.

When a patient is denying the seriousness of his illness, the minister can support him by encouraging him to express his feelings as this is necessary before he can accept the reality of his condition. He may continue to deny his illness and care must be taken not to support his denial or to cause him any further anxiety by attempting to confront him. To such an individual, the pastoral person might minister by saying, "Since you're here in bed and undressed, why not stay until tomorrow when your doctor will return and give you more information about your illness." or "I know you feel it's a waste of time being here, but if you stay in bed a little while longer, your doctor will be able to check your condition thoroughly and make sure that you're O.K."

During the acute phase of the illness, the religious may need to confirm the patient's suspicion that he is seriously ill and possibly will die. At this time the pastoral counselor affords the patient the opportunity to express his fears about dying or simply touches the person's hand to show him that someone cares. If the patient has any belief in God, the pastoral visitor speaks to him about God's goodness and love for man. A prayer at this time might be very appropriate, and if the patient is a Catholic, he probably will find great solace in receiving the sacraments. The patient might also benefit from the suggestion of making his sufferings valuable; for example, by asking God that through them peace would come to the world. When death is imminent, being with the patient and his family requires a deep sensitivity to human suffering. They are suffering, each in his own unique way. The patient who is dying, unable to express any of his feelings, needs a person near to support him. The clergyman sensitive to non-verbal behavior readily responds to the needs of the dying person who needs help to die, who feels helpless and lonely. The impact of his "aloneness" is terrifying and the religious counselor ministers principally by his concerned presence.

The pastoral visitor can help the patient who is angry or feeling guilty by encouraging him to verbalize his feelings without rejecting him. The patient needs assistance when he questions, "Why me?", or he feels, "What have I done to deserve this?" Empathetic listening is valuable as it allows the person to express his anger without any judgment being made. Travelbee states, "Ill persons who 'feel sorry for themselves' may be attempting to relate with others in the only way they are able to relate. Such individuals need understanding, not condemnation."[3] Guilt feelings arise from repressed anger and the lowering of one's self-worth. Listening to the patient voicing his fears concerning his future, offering alternate ways of coping, helps him adjust to his new and altered life. The patient needs support as he adapts to the changes resulting from his illness. His life style will be changed and he will be going home to a family that has changed. His family has made some adjustments during his absence and his going home will be an adjustment for the entire family who must now become involved in his convalescence.

Emotions of the Family of the Seriously Ill

When a seriously ill person is admitted to a critical care unit, the family waits anxiously outside the unit wondering what's going on inside. Since the doctor and the personnel are involved in the care of the patient, no one has any time at first to help the family deal with the "unknown." Racing through their minds are thoughts like, "Is he going to live or die? Will he ever be able to work again?" The family clearly faces uncertainty, and even after the doctor speaks with them they may be asking themselves these same questions because the doctor can't give them any definite information until the results of the tests come back or until 72 hours have passed.

Accompanying the feeling of uncertainty is one of isolation. The relatives don't know exactly what's going on in the unit; they don't kow if their loved one is getting better or worse, they don't know or can't understand the explanations concerning the many treatments that are being given. Separation has been forced on them. They are accustomed to being around their family member all the time and now are unable to see him even for a minute. They feel cut off, isolated from him. Sometimes a concerned relative waits in the visitors' area alone as other relatives may not have come yet, or possibly there may be no other relatives.

The anxiously waiting relatives usually feel completely helpless, too. Their loved one is in the unit and they are outside "doing absolutely nothing." It would relieve their anxiety if they could just do something for him, but they can't. All they can do is wait and hope and pray. At this point they realize their dependence on the doctor and the nursing staff. Everything seems to rest with them and the family must stand by helplessly as they perform their duties.

This helpless feeling is often followed by anger. The family would like to help but can't and so they become angry. They don't know why they are angry, but they simply feel it. Some families vent their anger on the staff, others on the doctor, others on the pastoral visitor because he represents God to them and others become angry at each other.

There are still others who become angry at the seriously ill patient. After all, if he would have been more careful this accident would not have occurred or if he would have gone to the doctor for regular checkups, the doctor could easily have prevented this heart attack. Another reason for becoming angry at the patient is that because of him the normal routine at home has been disrupted. Formerly, everybody enjoyed the evening meal together and after that they leisurely washed the dishes before sitting down to watch television. Now they have to rush home from work, eat a hurried meal and then go to the hospital. The whole family life pattern has been changed because of this loved one's illness, and it's natural for the family members to become angry at the patient but they are too embarrassed to admit it, even to themselves.

Intermingled with the anger is guilt. The family feels they may in some way have caused the serious illness. "If only I hadn't asked him to shovel the snow, this never would have happened." or "If I hadn't pushed him so hard to work overtime to pay off our new home, this heart attack wouldn't have happened." The family blames themselves for the sickness and when this becomes too uncomfortable, they shift the blame to the doctor for not detecting the illness earlier or to the nurses for not taking better care of the patient. Some family members feel very guilty because they have not visited their parent for a long time or haven't done some favor they promised to do months ago. These family members can become very demanding of the staff, constantly checking to make sure everything possible is being done for the patient and being critical when the call light is not answered immediately. After all, if the relative dies, they will find it difficult to live with their guilt and they transfer the guilt or the blame to the staff or the doctor.

In addition to these other feelings of guilt, the family could also feel remorseful because they are thinking of finances when their parent or aunt is critically ill in the unit. The thought of money, insurance, and a will seem so mercenary and cold that the family thinks they must put that thought out of their minds immediately. When the family cannot dispel these ideas, they feel very guilty and question the sincerity of their love for their critically ill relative.

Another feeling that families often experience is grief. They anticipate the death of their loved one and begin mourning their loss even before he has died. By doing this the family is trying to prepare themselves for the pain of loss and separation so that when death occurs it is not so painful. This behavior is natural but it should not be encouraged because the relative might not die. Then the family becomes angry at the patient for recovering since they were prepared to give him up and now will have to go through that a second time. A final worry of the relatives in the waiting area of the intensive care or the coronary unit concerns the dependent persons at home. They wonder who will take care of their children or their aged parent at home alone. Sometimes the concern is even about a pet who is very important to them.

Ministering to the Family of the Seriously Ill

Coming to know the patient as a person who is suffering, the pastoral visitor becomes involved in his total world. This allows the minister to become part of the ill person's family helping them to cope with the many feelings they are experiencing. Since serious sickness causes a major disruption in the family structure the relatives need assistance. The pastoral visitor can be of tremendous help to the family because he functions as a laison person between the health team and the family and between the patient and the family.

Those suffering from an abrupt change in their lives need to know that someone understands their difficulties. Most families need reassurance as they strive to accept the reality of the seriousness of their loved one's illness. The minister can give this effectively as well as encourage them to voice their different feelings.

The most immediate need of the family is to know what is happening to their relative. The pastoral person can obtain general information from the doctor and relay this to the family who often have jumped to the conclusion that the worst has happened. The "unknown" is painful in itself and it is helpful when the family is given some significant information. At this time it is beneficial to inform the family which doctors and other medical people are treating the patient. This will reassure them that everything possible is being done. To further reduce their anxieties, the religious counselor informs the family that the doctor knows they are waiting and as soon as he has time he will give them more details and be available to answer any questions they may have.

During the acute phase, the minister is available in case death comes quickly or the patient dies without regaining consciousness. The pastor is supportive to the family coping with the sudden death. Assisting the family to talk about their loss helps them to view the situation realistically and face it. Donna Aquilera explains that "family reaction to the death of a member develops in stages varying in time. The death of a loved one must produce an active expression of feeling in the normal course of events. Omission of such a reaction is to be considered as much a variation from the normal as is an excess in time and intensity. Unmanifested grief will be found expressed in some way or another; each new loss can cause grief for the current loss as well as reactivate the grieving process of previous episodes."[4] Ministers involved in any acute life-threatening situation with a patient and his family must have knowledge as well as expertise in crisis intervention. He must understand that every individual will react to death in his own way so knowledge of the grief process alone is not enough.

The pastoral visitor expects the family to express some anger at the hospital and staff and is prepared when they give way to their feelings. He realizes that the anger is not really directed against him and he does not take it personally. He does not attempt to defend the staff or hospital but remains neutral. He confines himself to indicating to the family that he understands the feelings they are experiencing. If the religious counselor becomes defensive he will only increase their anger. On the other hand, when the minister encourages the expression of their feelings, the hostility is usually diluted to some extent. After listening to the family's initial blast of hostility, the pastoral visitor might say, "All these things really make you angry." The family's reaction is, "Hey, this guy isn't against me. He's on my side. He understands how I feel."[5]

When the family hints they feel guilty about causing the sickness, the religious might say, "I wonder what you could have done to prevent it." Or, "Do you really think you have to take total responsibility for your husband's health?" Statements like these cause the family members to rethink their position and to work through their feelings. When the family whispers about the fact that someone ought to go down to the bank to see about switching the names on the bank books, the pastoral person might reflect, "I suppose it makes you feel embarrassed to think about such matters at a time like this." or, "I guess it seems kind of selfish to mention such things when your father is so sick." Again, the goal is to urge the family to understand their own feelings and thus be able to deal with them effectively. The minister goes on to reassure the family that these thoughts about finances are normal and that it is practical to take care of these matters. Sometimes, he might suggest legal assistance when the family is uncertain what they can do about finances at this time.

Because of these guilt feelings some families refuse to leave the critical care waiting areas even to go home for short periods of time. They can't stand the thought that their loved one might die when they are not present. The family usually find it comforting when the clergy reassures them that it's all right to go home for a little while because the nurses have their phone number and will call them if there is any change in the patient's condition. In addition, the pastoral visitor reminds them that their primary obligation is to care for their own psychological and physical health. This will enable them to relax a little more when they do go home.

A pastoral counselor is a significant member of the health team in critical care units. He is the most likely person to give support to the patient and his family in time of crisis. His position in the health team is flexible and he can assist both the patient and his family as they face a life-threatening situation. The pastoral visitor brings to the critically ill a special kind of expertise, that of giving spiritual comfort to those suffering and dying. Understanding their response to illness and what meaning it has for them gives the minister the opportunity to assist the sick to grow from their experience. It is not an easy task to help others to find meaning in that which seems so meaningless. The religious who develops interpersonal relationships provides the kind of assistance to the sick from which they can grow as persons. Travelbee describes it as, "Since every human being is unique it follows that meaning discovered in the experience of illness and suffering will be unique to the individual undergoing the experience. Because meaning can be detected only by the ill individual, it follows that health workers, family, or friends of the ill individual cannot give meaning to the ill person although they can help the person to arrive at meaning."[6]

NOTES

1. Janet Smith, R.N., M.S., "Adverse Effects of Critical Care Units," *Critical Care Nursing* (Philadelphia: J.B. Lippincott Company, 1973), p. 16.
2. Karen D. Busch, R.N., M.S. and Barbara M. Gallo, R.N., M.S., "Emotional Response to Illness," *Critical Care Nursing* (Philadelphia: J.B. Lippincott Company, 1973), p. 10.
3. Joyce Travelbee, *Interpersonal Aspects of Nursing* (Philadelphia: F.A. Davis Company, 1971), p. 147.
4. Donna C. Aquilera, R.N., M.S., *Crisis Intervention Theory and Methodology* (St. Louis: The C.V. Mosby Company, 1970), p. 82.
5. Gregg W., Downey, "The 'Crisis Minister' at Work: Reducing Hostility, Maintaining Dignity, and Controlling Emotions in the Emergency Room," *Modern Hospital*, September 1973, p. 86.
6. Travelbee, *op. cit.*, p. 162.

SELECTED BIBLIOGRAPHY

Elbert, Edmund J., *I Understand* (New York: Sheed and Ward, 1971).
Frank, K.A., *et al.*, "Long-Term Effects of Open-Heart Surgery on Intellectual Functioning," *Journal of Thoracic and Cardiovascular Surgery* 64, 5 (1972), p. 811.
———, "A Survey of Adjustment to Cardiac Surgery," *Archives of Internal Medicine* 130 (1972), p. 735.
Holland, Jimmie, *et al.*, "The ICU Syndrome: Fact or Fancy," *Psychiatry in Medicine* 4, 3 (1973), p. 241.
Kornfeld, Donald S., "Psychiatric Problems of an Intensive Care Unit," *Medical Clinics of North America* 55, 5 (1971), p. 1353.
Robinson, Lisa, R.N., M.S., Ph.D., *Psychological Aspects of the Care of Hospitalized Patients* (Philadelphia: F.A. Davis Company, 1972).
Switzer, David K., *Minister as Crisis Counselor* (Nashville: Abingdon Press, 1974).

7. Ministering to the Geriatric Patient

Sometimes when you and I bend over to pick something up from the floor we groan as we straighten up. At this time we realize we are growing older. Not only are we growing older, but our population today is growing older because more and more people are living longer. In 1971 there were almost 20 million persons over age 65 which means that about 10% of the population belonged to that category. In 1975 there are more than 22 million elderly. In addition to that, the elderly population itself is getting older. Several years ago, 4,574 persons receiving social security benefits were 100 or more years old and more than 7 million of the 20 million elderly were 75 or older. By 1980 it is estimated there will be 9 million persons over 75 years old.[1]

This increase in the aged in our country is supported by insurance statistics which indicate that the life span has increased greatly in the last 50 years. Today, the average age for women is 74.6 and for men 67.1. This is a drastic change from 1920 when the average age for men was 53.6 and for women 54.6.[2]

Ideally, these millions of older people are experiencing meaningful lives and are assured of a fulfilling and satisfying old age. Ideally, too, the elderly are understood and esteemed by their loved ones and their different psychological, social and spiritual needs are being met. Realistically, this is not happening often because modern society seems to have no real place for them. Much of their accumulated wisdom is no longer of value in guiding the young because the world has changed so much. Consequently, they frequently feel aimless, bored, unneeded, and a burden.

In this article I will indicate four important needs of the elderly person and give some ideas on how these needs may be met. They are: a need for understanding by being aware of his losses, his psychological needs, his sociological needs and his spiritual needs.

I
LOSSES OF THE ELDERLY

Loss of Memory and Perceptual Efficiency

We are given insight into the world of the elderly person by understanding the many losses he has suffered. Usually the senior citizen undergoes the loss of his recent memory. He remembers things that occurred in his childhood or when he was working, but has difficulty recalling the visitors he had yesterday or what he ate for lunch today. He experiences the loss of perceptual efficiency. His hearing is not as good as it used to be, nor is his eyesight. His voluntary responses are slowed down because the speed at which the association of ideas proceeds is reduced. The central integrating power in the aged person is diminished, with the result that he cannot interpret and integrate the limited amount of stimuli he is perceiving from the environment.[3]

Narcissistic Losses

Narcissistic losses which take place in the elder of extreme importance. One of the first losses of this nature that occurs in women is menopause which means for some the loss of function as a woman. Unfortunately, shortly after this, many mothers receive a second narcissistic loss, the loss of the children from the parental home. Children leaving home for college and/or getting married present a difficult adjustment for mothers because they were significant persons who had a distinct sense of being useful and needed while the children were at home. Fathers experience some difficulty adjusting to the loss of the children too, but normally not as much as the mothers. A more difficult loss men must face is the gradual decreasing sexual potency, and with the emphasis today on sexual performance, this is a severe loss for many men. In both sexes, one of the most stressful events experienced by the elderly is the loss of their spouse. This is especially severe if the children have already left home and the aged person is forced to fend for himself.[4]

Another loss is retirement which means that the income is greatly reduced, that he loses his status as a wage earner, and possibly also the status as foreman of the shop or the wife loses her status as secretary to some executive. In our society retirement is a significant loss because achievement through work has been the criterion of worth. As a result the elderly themselves, as well as younger people, equate worklessness with worthlessness.[5]

As the senior citizen becomes older, he gradually loses his independence. He relies more and more on his children for help: taking care of the garden, shopping for groceries, driving him to the doctor, etc. Thus, roles gradually become reversed. The parent loses his independence by becoming dependent on his children for all kinds of help, and this role reversal is very difficult for many to accept.

When an elderly person becomes senile or very feeble, he faces the loss of more independence for he either moves in with one of his children or takes up residence in a nursing home and no matter which move he makes, he relinquishes the freedom that maintaining one's own home affords. Many senior citizens dread the thought of going to a nursing home because to them it represents a place where old people are put away and forgotten, a place where people receive very poor care, a place where people go to die. If the person is encouraged to voice his feelings about nursing homes and to participate in the selection of a home the transfer may be made with less trauma. Realistically though, it must be admitted that some senior citizens are too senile to make any decisions and only become frustrated when they are asked to do so.

An older person usually finds the adjustment to a nursing home very difficult. The meals which are naturally different from home cooking are served at a definite time every day and can't be adjusted to fit the resident's TV schedule. Baths are taken daily, and if assistance is needed, the bath often occurs at the convenience of the staff rather than the resident. In addition, now he has only one room or possibly shares a room with someone else whereas before he had a four or five room home for himself. Thus, when a man or a woman enters a nursing home, he or she loses a great deal of freedom and independence.

Usually, it takes several weeks before a person can become comfortable in a nursing home, and during this adjustment period everything imaginable will be wrong with the home i.e., the food, the temperature in the room, the unfriendly manner of the nurses, aides, and the other residents, etc. If a minister of pastoral care takes the time to listen to these complaints with empathy, and then indirectly questions as to whether there was any other solution possible considering all the person's disabilities, it eases the adjustment period. Once the elderly person is finally settled in the home, he seldom complains and when he does, his complaints are a ploy the aged use to test if the religious visitor is still concerned about him.[6]

One 86 year old woman who was living in a nursing home and had to be taken in a wheelchair wherever she went expressed her losses in this conversation with her pastor:

Woman: Before I lived in my own place and was able to get out a little bit with my crutches. It was difficult but I made it. Now I can't do anything by myself. If I want to go down to the chapel, I have to call a nurse to help me.

Pastor: It's painful being so dependent on others.

Woman: Yes, before I could do a lot of things on my own, and I hate to bother those nurses so much. They're busy with other people who are much worse off than I am.

Pastor: It's this helpless feeling that gets one down.

Woman: Yes, this is terrible. (She begins crying softly and there is a brief period of silence as the pastor clasps her hand.)

Pastor: This hurts you deeply.

Woman: It sure does, and it's not only hard being stuck in this room either. Before, I could read. I always liked reading. I planned on doing a lot of reading when I retired. I enjoy *Reader's Digest*. But now I can't read some days. The print is just blurred. Look at this newspaper (showing the paper to her pastor). I can only read the headlines, but can't read any of the articles because the print is too small.

Pastor: This prevents you from keeping up with all the news.

Woman: It wouldn't be so bad if I could hear good. But you know my hearing is poor too. I can understand you because you talk slowly and you're looking directly at me. It's a different story with the TV programs. Those newscasters talk fast and the speaker seems to be poor. I can't understand everything they say. I catch about every third word. Boy, it's not easy getting old.

Pastor: You have suffered a lot of losses in the last few years, and it's very difficult adjusting to all of them.

Woman: It's tough and nobody knows what you're going through either. I look at the clock and think ten minutes have passed and only five minutes have gone by. Time really goes slow when you have nothing you can do.

Pastor: Because of all of these losses and because nobody seems to understand, you feel like you're living in a world by yourself.

Reactions to These Losses

When an oldster experiences difficulty in accepting all these losses, he uses two common defense mechanisms, projection and denial. With the gradual awareness of his increasing inability to perform as he once did, he is inclined to project his own shortcomings to others. One elderly lady, for example, frequently misplaced her glasses and couldn't remember where she left them. Instead of admitting that it was her fault, she claimed her roommate stole them. When a senior citizen projects the blame on another person, it indicates he is unable to cope with the fact he is slipping. This projection causes him to appear suspicious and paranoid. In addition, oldsters are extremely sensitive to any rejection, real or imagined, and this tends to make them even more suspicious of everything that happens to them.

A 77 year old lady living in a nursing home, for example, lost her false teeth and immediately called the nurse saying that someone had stolen them. The nurse looked everywhere, but could not find the teeth. A week later one of the nurses was in the chapel looking for a particular hymn book and under one of the benches in a corner she saw an object she couldn't quite identify. When she reached down to pick it up, she realized that these were the "lost" teeth. The lady had put them there for safe keeping during the Sunday service.

Unfortunately, the elderly parent often becomes very suspicious of the family member who has done the most for him. He accuses this devoted and faithful son or daughter of taking things from him and of being interested only in his money. Naturally, this hurts the devoted relative deeply, and the pastoral care minister assists by pointing out that the aged person is coping with his losses in this way. The aged parent chooses to become very paranoid of the relative who comes every day to visit because he feels this faithful child will not reject him and will continue coming in spite of his projection. On the other hand, when the child comes who hasn't made any attempt to visit for years, the aged parent will be most pleasant and loving because he feels he must. If he begins accusing the disinterested child of lack of attention, or of being concerned only for his money, he fears that this will be his last visit.

Another reason for the suspicious and paranoid conduct of the aged, is his impairment in hearing. Usually he can understand when he is spoken to directly. However, if a group of people are talking together in the background, all that he will hear is a confused mumble. Rather than admit that his hearing is failing, he frequently imagines that others are talking about him and possibly plotting against him.[7]

The senior citizen makes extensive use of the defense mechanism of denial when faced with severe stress. The older person can't cope with a problem and so he denies that it real'y exists. When he becomes concerned with his advancing years, illness and possible death, he uses every means at his disposal to deny the present difficult situation. Perhaps the most extensive use of denial is seen following the death of the spouse. A 70 year old man, for example, was admitted to a mental health institute because of confusion following the death of his wife. Such a great loss resulted in too stressful a situation for him to face so he solved the problem by convincing himself his wife had never really died.[8]

II
PSYCHOLOGICAL NEEDS

It is evident, then, that the old adult is psychologically as different from the young adult as the child is from the grown man. The elderly individual is a unique personality who requires special consideration to fill his many needs.[9] Three of his psychological needs are: meaning in life, security for himself and his possessions, and a sense of belonging.

Meaning in Life

One of the key problems of aging people is the frightening thought that there is no meaning to life anymore. When man becomes aware of the gradual decrease in his physical and mental powers, he begins to fear that he has become useless and unwanted. Many old people express their feelings of lack of purpose and meaning in phrases like: "I am no good for anything anymore." or "I am useless and not needed anymore."

There is no set meaning for all aged people because each human being must find his own meaning. Even though the meaning of existence is unique for each individual, it is not invented but discovered. The role of the pastoral minister is to broaden the person's field of vision and to help him become aware of the whole wide spectrum of meaning and values. The minister begins his search with the person for meaning in life by drawing from his religious beliefs and then strives to find other meanings from his interests, daily influences, etc.[10]

In other words, the elderly must become emotionally involved with someone or some project in order to continue to find meaning in life. It is not sufficient for him to be involved only with his children because then he just sits around waiting for them to visit and complains when they don't come as frequently as he thinks they should.[11]

A number of elderly people have made a beautiful adjustment. Dr. Ernest Hirsch, a psychologist at the Menninger Foundation, recently surveyed 100 people over the age of 70 and asked only one question: "What years do you consider the best years of life?" The majority felt that the 40's and 50's were the best years of life. However, 25% found an added meaning in life in their old age. They reasoned they were living in the best years of their lives because their major obligations in life had been fulfilled. Old age to them represented a time to relax and enjoy life. Travel was mentioned frequently as one of the pleasures of old age.[12]

There are other examples of well-adjusted senior citizens. A 93 year old lady who has been a resident in a nursing home for 13 years has become emotionally involved in a project—making doll clothes. These clothes are raffled at the annual bazaar which the nearby hospital sponsors every November and so she feels she is contributing something to an institution she loves. Another lady at the same home makes herself feel needed and useful by frequently knitting dishcloths which she sells or enjoys giving to others as presents.

Dr. Victor Frankl, the author of the popular book *Man's Search For Meaning*, illustrates this concept of discovering some meaning in life by recalling a fellow prisoner at the Auschwitz prison camp who had decided to commit suicide because he had suffered enough. Frankl reminded him of his child waiting to be reunited with him—someone for whom he was irreplaceable and this enabled the man to persevere in spite of the pain he was undergoing. Thus the thought of his child gave meaning to his life.[13]

Recently the researchers at the Center for the Study of Aging and Human Development at Duke University voiced the same idea saying that the attitude of the older person influences his behavior greatly. "The decision to have an active mental, physical, and social life is really an important decision," says Dr. Eric Pfeiffer one of the researchers at the Duke Center. "It's a yea-saying to life."[14] It's the function of a good samaritan to struggle with the elderly to find some "why" for living so he can still possess a zest for life.

Security for Himself and His Possessions

If the senior citizen continues living in his own home, he fears for his safety. He realizes his hearing and sight are failing and questions his ability to detect the presence of an intruder in his home. His lack of security is aggravated when he reads in the paper or sees on TV that some older person was attacked and his home burglarized. One older woman who lives alone is so fearful of being robbed that she never turns on her radio or TV. When she was asked her reason for not tuning in some programs, she replied: "I'm afraid to. If the radio or TV are on, then I couldn't hear if someone was breaking in." As a result of this overwhelming fear, this lonely woman is by herself all day and never is informed of what's happening in the world except by the newspaper.

Other oldsters express their lack of a sense of security by constantly being afraid of falling. They fear breaking a hip and becoming hospitalized or possibly permanently incapacitated. Hence, they are especially careful not to wax their floors at all or only slightly and also are careful not to fall on uneven cement or to stumble over a "throw" rug.

If the geriatric person is residing in a nursing home, the underlying fear is still a sense of insecurity in spite of the fact that adequate safety features are demanded by federal and state laws today. Although safety devices are permanent installments, staff members often do not encourage patients to use them or do not explain and train patients in their use. A brusk voice, a workmanlike awareness of the passage of time and a curt manner by the staff are sometimes substituted for a clear explanation and a soft voice of encouragement to utilize them. A helpful Christian in visiting the senior citizen is aware of his uncertainty and tries to establish a climate of openness and warmth by a congenial manner so that the person feels free to express any of his fears and doubts.[15]

In addition to the feelings of insecurity about his personal safety, the aged person worries about his possessions which many other people view as being of little value because of their age, use, and lack of modern style. However, to the senior citizen these possessions are very valuable because he has many emotional ties to them. Possibly, this dress or chair was given to an elderly widow by her husband, and it reminds her of his devoted love.

If an elderly parent moves in with one of his children or into a nursing home, a problem usually arises about his personal belongings. He values them highly but can't take all of them with him. Mementoes, trinkets, clothing and familiar articles of furniture provide security symbols and links with the past. A good samaritan, preparing him to move, urges him to express his feelings of pain and loss as he separates himself from some of these treasured articles.

Staff members of a nursing home often prefer to see the resident's room stripped of all but the bare essentials to make their job of cleaning easier. Sometimes a daughter-in-law wishes her father-in-law would get rid of some of his "junk," the old faded pictures and other mementoes because these make dusting twice as difficult. Yet it is important to remember the value he places on them. An alert visitor notes these articles and discovers that the elderly talk with great eagerness about them.[16]

Sense of Belonging

When an older person cuts the last ties of a former existence by leaving the familiar surroundings of his home and enters into the unfamiliar, he often feels he doesn't belong anymore; he no longer counts; he no longer is an individual. He's just a burden that has to be cared for.[17]

Every person lives in relation to his environment. His manner and its expression depend not on him alone but on others around him. If the tendency of his family or the staff of a nursing home is to constrain and rule him, to treat him as if he is in his second childhood, then he readily feels he doesn't belong. He feels he's a guest, an outsider, a thing to be taken care of. On the other hand, if he is encouraged to participate in the planning of his placement in a nursing home or in the activities of his day he will more readily feel that he belongs.

When the family or the staff of a nursing home discourages his attempts to create a place for himself, the oldster tends to withdraw and as a result becomes lonely and isolated. These feelings increase his sense of insecurity, and re-emphasize his unacceptability and loneliness. The role of the pastoral care minister is to support and encourage him to become integrated into his new surroundings.

III
SOCIOLOGICAL NEEDS

Need for Success

Every person needs to experience success from time to time for good mental health and this need is accentuated in old age. An oldster feels a sense of accomplishment by performing simple routine acts such as bathing and feeding himself, tending to his clothes, dusting and straightening his room. Relatives or the staff at a nursing home could easily perform these tasks much more quickly, but in so doing they deprive him of contributing to the orderliness of his living quarters as well as of achieving some personal satisfaction through the performance of these simple acts.

A senior citizen who is sick experiences this sense of achievement when an observant pastoral care minister notes some progress toward recovery, or simply that he is holding his own in the survival contest. A good samaritan visiting a senior citizen, for example, comments on the improvement the elderly person has made in walking with the cane. "You seem to move around the room better today than you did before." A compliment like this gives the elderly encouragement to continue trying because he often becomes depressed if he does not feel there is any progress or very little. Since small gains provide more satisfactions than large gains widely spaced, an alert minister urges him to establish realistic goals so he can attain them. When he experiences success, he is motivated to continue trying.

Need for Recognition

Recognition, another need present in every human being, increases as a person ages because he feels no one values him or his contributions anymore. He needs to be recognized formally and accepted as an individual possessing unique characteristics. This recognition is provided when a good samaritan comments favorably on his attempts to venture into any kind of activity and praises him for successfully completing some task. It is profitable to have this recognition and acclaim shared with all the people who care for and visit him.

Taking an interest in the senior citizen as a person with a unique past history also gives him recognition. So it's beneficial if the pastoral care minister inquires about his former employment, grandchildren, etc., without probing into any of his personal affairs. A little knowledge of his past makes him very different from all of the others and makes him feel accepted as an individual.

When a good samaritan offers recognition, he acknowledges the self-image of the older person and indicates that he still has a unique identity. The aged person experiences a loss of identity as he becomes disassociated from his friends and family, and separated from familiar surroundings. Confusion contributes to this loss of identity. He may often question who he is, where he is, and why he is there. Calm acceptance of bewilderment, clear explanations and answers to questions, and a climate of acceptance of the individual as he is and as he sees himself are helpful reassurances an alert Christian provides.[18]

The most common manner of recognizing another person's individuality is calling him by his proper name. This clearly distinguishes him from every other human being. Sometimes nicknames are given to an aged person, but this is generally avoided because they often detract from his dignity as a person. In using a person's first name an alert Christian is careful not to speak in a condescending tone. Without realizing it one can easily fall into the habit of speaking down to an elderly person. For example, in one nursing home a 74 year old man is called "Billy" as if he were a little boy.

Need for Association

God created human beings as social persons and this aspect of human nature is not lost in old age. So a senior citizen is encouraged to associate with others by eating in a common room, by recreating with a group and by sitting with others. It takes a lot of effort for an aged person to walk or get into a wheel chair and so frequently he prefers just to sit in his room doing nothing. He needs encouragement to put forth this effort to mingle with others in order that he doesn't withdraw into himself.

The oldster can strike up friendships with others because of mutual interests, common goals, common past experiences or simply common loneliness. No matter what the cause of the association, it is necessary and profitable because it gives him an opportunity to share his thoughts and feelings with others, and maybe allow him to become emotionally involved in the welfare of another person.[19]

IV
SPIRITUAL NEEDS

The Existence of Spiritual Needs

In addition to these other needs, many studies have verified the fact that the elderly also have spiritual needs. Dr. Edgar Jackson emphasized this point at the Annual Conference of Pastors stating that there is no area in psychiatry where religion is more important than that branch of psychiatry which deals with the problems associated with the process of aging. As people grow older they become more concerned with the problem of finding a meaning for their lives. As they look back over the years, they raise the questions of "why" and "wherefore." They become more concerned with the problem of existence and death suddenly becomes a reality which has to be considered as an imminent event. As a result of these experiences, many turn to God and religion and seek forgiveness of their sins.[20]

It is true that church attendance decreases because of the infirmities of extreme old age, but religious programs on radio and television increase as a substitute. Since most older people grew up in an era when spiritual needs were closely identified with organized religion, they usually look to their church and clergyman, not to the physician, the social worker or recreation leader, when they feel a need for religious support.[21]

Unfortunately, older members often are hesitant in seeking aid from the church because they feel that it does not give them meaningful roles anymore, that it is preoccupied with the younger people and that it ignores their opinions. The church seems to make little effort to reach out to them, for example, by offering them transportation if they need it to attend Mass. Instead, it excuses them from attendance and thus shuts them out further from participation in the community.

The Sacramental Needs

In an attempt to satisfy the spiritual needs of the elderly

Roman Catholics, the minister of pastoral care makes the celebration of the Eucharistic Sacrifical Meal available frequently, brings Holy Communion often to those who are bedfast, and provides an opportunity periodically to receive the sacraments of Penance and the Anointing of the Sick.

Many aged people have not been able to participate at Mass in years and consider it a privilege to have Mass celebrated in their home. It is surprising how well many of the elderly adapt to the new liturgy, if it is explained kindly and simply and the celebrant indicates by his actions that he is convinced of its value. At least many of them will co-operate, and this should not be too surprising since these people were reared in an era when the priest's word was respected and what he said was law. Surely, it is expected that some will still recite their rosary and say their novena prayers during Mass, but many will accept "Father's" wishes. The pastoral minister enlists the aid of the laity in preparing the "home Mass" including setting up the altar after giving them some instructions.

The liturgy offers some opportunities to fill spiritual as well as other needs. The offertory procession, for example, is an excellent opportunity for making them feel important and needed. When they present the water and the wine or the ciborium they feel they are contributing something special to the Mass and as a result that day will be significant in their week. Some also enjoy the "sign of peace." This is a beautiful time for them to soothe the arguments that may have arisen and also to receive a personal greeting from the priest, a gesture they always consider a privilege.

Every opportunity ought to be given to those who cannot participate in the Eucharistic celebration to receive Communion frequently—even daily, especially during the Easter season. Those who care for the sick may also receive Communion with them, providing the usual requirements of the Eucharistic fast are fulfilled.[22]

Since the bedfast can receive Communion at any hour, an atmosphere of recollection can be created by having a specified time for Communion. Receiving the sacraments need not be a somber experience; rather, it should be a joyful celebration.

However, the joy should be a joy in the Lord, not in the afternoon ball game, since the sacraments are privileged moments of a personal meeting with Christ.

Surely, the pastoral care minister understands that when the aged person receives Communion, he has an excellent opportunity to seek the graces he needs to bear up in a Christ-like manner with the difficulties he experiences in daily living. A byproduct of participating in this sacrament is that the person realizes he is still part of the worshiping community of his church and has not been forgotten. If the priest has a number of Communion calls in his parish, lay distributors of Communion could assist him in meeting the needs of the shut-ins.

It is not necessary to stress the fact that if the person cannot distinguish between table bread and the consecrated host, he should not be permitted to receive Communion. This applies especially to the senile, but since they have lucid moments, the decision as to when they can receive is best made in consultation with a nurse on a day to day basis, keeping in mind that Christ instituted the sacraments for the benefit of all of his people.[23]

It is not enough for a child to know his mother loves him. If she doesn't put her arms around him, he will never be sure of her love. So Christ, accommodating himself to human nature offers the Sacrament of Reconciliation so that man can be visibly reassured of Christ's forgiveness. Even though the senior citizen may have sinned only venially, he often finds comfort in this tangible proof of reconciliation.

After all, he realizes he is getting closer to death and wants reassurance that he is prepared to meet his Lord. In addition, the elderly were trained to go to confession monthly or every time they received Communion. Consequently, many of them like to be reassured of the heavenly Father's forgiveness on a regular basis.[24]

The Second Vatican Council preferred the name Anointing of the Sick to Extreme Unction and said that as soon as one of the faithful appears to be in danger of death from sickness or old age, he should receive the graces of this sacrament.[25] The crisis of serious illness can come quickly as in the case of a stroke or heart attack, but most often with the aged there is no marked change but a gradual, almost imperceptible decline which can be noticed first by the nurses who care for them day after day. The pastoral minister who works closely with the medical and nursing staff of any nursing home can request them to report these vital changes to him so that the aged person can be anointed when he is conscious and can participate fully in the graces of the sacrament. The thought of being anointed frightens some elderly people who still regard it as "last rites." The minister could help to prevent any unnecessary fear by clearly explaining the purpose of the sacrament before anointing.

In administering the anointing an effort should be made to capture the spirit of St. James who indicated in his epistle the interest of the whole community in the welfare of the sick.[26] It is fitting, then, to administer the sacrament when the family or members of the community are present. The presence of others is a sign that the Christian community stands by the aging with genuine loving concern. It is equally a sign of the continuing love and presence of Christ, faithful in sickness and in health. Through this sacrament he is present to the elderly person just as truly as he was to the suffering men and women of Galilee and Judea. He asks of the elderly now exactly what he asked of Jarius: "Do not be afraid; only have faith."

Along the streets of Nazareth and Jerusalem some were cured of their illnesses, others were given courage and patience to find meaning and hope in the shadows of life. So today, the power of Christ brings healing to those who receive this sacrament with faith, sometimes physical healing or improvement, other times renewed hope, and insight into the deeper meaning of suffering. Furthermore, Christ reminds the recipients of the anointing that until those happy days of heaven: "My grace is enough for you, power is at its best in weakness."[27]

If the sacrament is understood in this way, it becomes a joyful, comforting experience, reminding the aged person that Christ and we Christians still love him and that old age offers privileged moments of Christian growth. Anointing a group of the aged at Mass or outside of Mass contributes to creating this desired atmosphere.

Sometimes, the aged who haven't been to church for a long

time seem very hardened in their path of irreligion. The pastoral minister maintains interest in these "hopeless cases" because a number of them are eager to return to their creator when they realize they are dying. Dr. Byron Stinson, an assistant professor of psychiatry at Ohio State University, supports this thought because he feels that people adopt the values they had as children when they begin to die. Since most people have had some type of religious training, they feel the dying are generally anxious to have assistance in relating to their Maker. From his experience it doesn't seem to matter if they have not prayed or gone to church for years, for they still usually accept the faith of their youth at this time.[28]

Other Spiritual Needs

It is not sufficient simply to provide opportunities for the aged to encounter Christ in the sacraments. At times they need spiritual advice and at other times they need to meet Christ in the person of someone who is really concerned about them and takes an interest in their welfare. Programs should be devised which encourage the widest possible participation of all the parishioners, since it is the concern of all the members of a parish community to care for those in special need. Soliciting the aid of youth groups, high school and university students, and church societies in visiting the elderly is very valuable. Many such groups bring gifts at Christmas and sing carols, but the sad fact is that these old people are forgotten during the rest of the year. The pastoral minister would provide a much needed service if he could urge any group to take a continual interest in visiting the aged in the nursing homes or in their own private homes. Often, a group will begin such a task with great enthusiasm, but their interest will die gradually because the members have not worked through their own feelings about becoming old. So the minister urges them to express their feelings on this subject. He can also stimulate interest in this work by discussing with the members the needs of the senior citizens and how they are contributing to meet these needs.

Simple instructions on basic pastoral approaches are made available to those who engage in visiting so that they know the most effective ways of speaking about the faith and praying with the aged. It is expected that the pastoral minister will aid in organizing this wide-based participation and give the program the benefit of his experience and leadership. Naturally, part of this leadership requires continued personal involvement in the visitation program thereby insuring their availability especially to those who are dying.[29]

A final thought in regard to meeting the religious needs of the aged concerns prayer. Popular belief has it that the elderly can now pray more because they have so much leisure time at their disposal. This is simply not true because the elderly often complain about their loss of concentration and inability to keep awake. As a result, they are at times plagued by guilt feelings in this regard and the priest can help alleviate these by listening and later giving assurances that God understands their good intentions and loves them dearly.

NOTES

1. White House Conference on Aging, U.S. Department of Health, Education and Welfare, Washington, D.C., 1971.

2. *1972 Life Insurance Fact Book*, Institute of Life Insurance, New York, N.Y.

3. Schoenberg, Carr, Peretz, and Kutscher, "Reaction to Loss in the Aged," *Loss And Grief* (New York: Columbia University Press, 1970), pp. 199-204.

4. Edgar B. Jackson, M.D., "Religion, Psychiatry and the Geriatric Patient," Annual Conference of Pastors, Osawatomie, Kansas, November, 1959.

5. White House Conference on Aging.

6. Sister Maria Jude, O. Carm., "Pastoral Care to the Aging," Minneapolis, Minnesota, National Association of Catholic Chaplains' Convention, June 1969.

7. Felix Post, M.D., "Paranoid Disorders in the Elderly," *Postgraduate Medicine*, April 1973, Vol. 53, p. 53.

8. Edgar B. Jackson, M.D., *op. cit.*

9. Wilma Donahue, "Psychologic Aspects in Management of the Geriatric Patient," in E.V. Cowdry (ed), *The Care Of The Geriatric Patient* (St. Louis: The C.V. Mosby Company, 1958), p. 27.

10. Alfons Deeken, *Growing Old and How To Cope With It* (New York: Paulist Press, 1972), pp. 68-73.

11. David W. Sprague, M.D., "Care of the Aged," Masonic Home, Springfield, Ohio, February 21, 1972.

12. Ann Landers, *Springfield Sun*, March 9, 1973.

13. Viktor Frankl, M.D., "Man in Search of Meaning," Urbana College, Urbana, Ohio, January 26, 1972.

14. "Tips on How To Stay Young," *Newsweek*, April 16, 1973, p. 66.

15. Margaret Fenn, D.B.A., "Non-Physical Needs of the Geriatric Patient," *Hospital Progress*, December 1967, pp. 48-54.

16. *Perspectives on Aging Series*, Concept Media, Costa Mesa, California, 1973.

17. Monroe Mitchel, J.A.H.A., "Chaplains and Long-Term Care," August 16, 1970, Vol. 44, Part 1.

18. Margaret Fenn, *op. cit.*

19. Monroe Mitchel, *op. cit.*

20. Edgar B. Jackson, *op. cit.*

21. 1971 White House Conference on Aging.

22. "Rites for the Sick," International Committee on English in the Liturgy, Inc., 1971, Washington, D.C.

23. Sister Maria Jude, *op. cit.*

24. Rev. Leonard Foley, O.F.M., *Signs of Love*, St. Anthony Messenger Press, Cincinnati, Ohio, 1971, pp. 158-159.

25. *Constitution on the Sacred Liturgy*, December 4, 1963, n. 73.

26. James 5:14.

27. 2 Corinthians 12:9.

28. Byron Stinson, M.D., "Recognition and Therapy of Depression," Ohio Medical Education Network, January 12, 1972.

SELECTED BIBLIOGRAPHY

Brantl, Virginia and Sr. Marie R. Brown, eds., *Readings in Gerontology* (St. Louis: Mosby, 1973).

Butler, Robert N., *Old Age In America* (New York: Harper & Row, 1974).

Faber, Heije and Ebel Van der Schoot, *The Art of Pastoral Conversation* (New York: Abingdon Press, 1965).

Moss, Bertram B., *Caring for the Aged* (Garden City, N.Y.: Doubleday, 1966).

Smith, Bert K., *Aging in America* (Boston: Beacon Press, 1973).

Vedder, Clyde B., *Gerontology: A Book of Readings* (Springfield, Ill: C.C. Thomas, 1971).

Wolff, Kurt, *Emotional Rehabilitation of the Geriatric Patient* (Springfield, Ill.: C.C. Thomas, 1971).

8. Ministering to the Terminally Ill

Americans live in a culture which says in many ways that if you are going to do anything as unpatriotic as to die, don't do it around me. Go to a special institution. Go live in some far-off city or take a long trip and don't come back, but don't just lay there and die. It makes me too uncomfortable.

It is not surprising that Americans have a difficult time dealing with death when a person considers that the whole culture emphasizes the value of life and the beauty of youth. The cosmetic industry is booming in this country and so are the industries which produce hair pieces, wigs and hair dye. We must look young at all costs because if we begin to show our age. We might have to face the fact that some day we will die and be annihilated.

A switchboard operator of a medium size hospital spoke of another evidence of our uncomfortableness with getting older and dying. She mentioned that people frequently call and request the hospital's insurance office without realizing that there are at least four: blue cross, commercial, medicaid and medicare. Whenever their voices indicated they were about 65, she suggested that they wanted to speak to the medicare office. A number of these people became very irritated that anyone would think they were old enough to benefit from medicare.

Another foible is the fact that in America the word death is seldom used. Instead, people speak of "when dad was with us" or "before we lost our father." Euphemisms are used because it is too painful to speak of death or a loved one being dead. The personnel of a hospital are not exempt from this uncomfortableness either. In one hospital, for example, the personnel never use the word "die" and instead always refer to the patient as having "expired." It appears they are hiding behind professional terminology because it leaves them feeling less anxious.

There are three major reasons for this uneasiness with the topic of death: the medical advances, the customs of our country, and a lack of faith in a life after death. As the statistics from a previous chapter have indicated, longevity has greatly increased. A few hundred years ago, death in infancy and early childhood was frequent, and there were few families who escaped losing a member of the family at an early age. Epidemics and plagues were common. Now, thanks to the advances in medicine, this has changed greatly in the last decades. Widespread vaccinations have practically eradicated many illnesses, at least in the United States. The use of antibiotics has contributed to an ever decreasing number of fatalities from infectious diseases. Prenatal clinics and education have effectly lowered the infant mortality rate.[1]

Thus the medical field though it has brought many blessings to our society with its achievements has also brought two bad effects. First, the American people have been led to believe they are immortal, that they will be spared from death by some medicine or operation. Second, in order to attain this success, medicine has devoted all of its attention to healing the sick while at the same time it has neglected the care of the dying. As a result, doctors are generally unprepared to deal with the dying patient for they have had no training in engaging in the death watch. In fact, this term seems almost unheard of today. The clergy too, until recently, have been equally unprepared to help the dying person, for the seminary curriculum did not provide any training in dealing with the dying person. Since the doctors and the clergy offered so little assistance to the dying, it is no wonder that people fear death and find it difficult to face it as part of life.[2]

The customs in our country surrounding death hinder us in coping with it. The overwhelming majority of deaths occur outside the home, most of them in some institution. The wake takes place in a funeral home instead of the home where the deceased lived often for many years, and in addition the embalmers use cosmetics to give an appearance of sleep and not death. As a result, death is something that happens out there to other people. It's not part of our lives as is the case with people of other countries. In Mexico, for example, the wake takes place in the home and the dead are usually not embalmed nor made to appear to be asleep. These customs help to convey to those people the fact that death is part of life, that it is something to be expected, something that every human being must face sometime.

Twenty-five years ago a strong belief in a life after death existed among the people of this land. The majority of the people believed in God and hoped to be united with him in heaven one day. Now, many Americans are not only questioning the existence of heaven and hell, but doubting the very existence of God. Hence, in the dying process many people no longer are supported by a strong faith, no longer comforted by the thought that the Lord who is their shepherd will always support them. Attendance at churches of almost every denomination has decreased drastically during the last ten years. This indicates a weakness of faith among our American people and accounts for their inability to rely upon God for help during their time of greatest need.

Should a Fatally Ill Person Be Told?

Considering the uneasiness of the American people in dealing with death, a question naturally arises: Should a terminally ill patient be informed of his condition? Certainly the doctor should tell the patient the truth; nevertheless, the approach to each person must be individualized. There is no standard formula for imparting this information. The situation calls for a gentle revelation, remembering that the most important aspect is not what the patient is told, but how he is told. The doctor who has the obligation and privilege of imparting this information does it, not in a brutal way, but rather in a manner that imparts useful information so as to dispel the fearful shadow of the unknown.[3]

Communicating the truth can be done in stages and need not be viewed as an all or none process. During the various phases of his illness, the patient's openness helps to determine how much detail the physician gives him. Once the patient has been told the nature of his sickness and the general prognosis, then the possibility of talking frankly about death has been admitted. This does not mean that such a conversation will necessarily take place, but it does mean that the whole atmosphere is changed. C.M. Saunders feels that at this point "we are free to wait quietly for clues from each patient, seeing them as individuals from whom we can expect intelligence, courage, and decisions."[4]

Some doctors and family members think that the patient should only be told about his condition, if he directly asks about it. This approach seems reasonable because it presumes the patient is an adult and will ask about his diagnosis if he really wants to know. Often though, the patient wishes to know about his condition and simply presumes the doctor will inform him when he has all the information from the tests or the biopsy. At other times the patient wants to know, but doesn't have the courage to ask directly. So he will ask indirectly in many different ways. For example, he will wonder out loud why he is getting weaker, why the pain is persisting, why his abdomen is becoming distended.

Dr. Thomas Hackett, a psychiatrist from Boston Massachusetts General Hospital, often openly informs the patient of his potentially fatal diagnosis and then assures him that he will receive the best medical assistance available, that he will prevent pain as much as possible, that no one knows what medical discoveries will be made that will save his life, or when the present medicine might take effect, and therefore he cannot predict the time of death.[5]

As a member of the healing team, the pastoral minister works with the doctors and nurses and makes his unique contribution by urging the person to make the most of the time he has left and not just to give up and retreat into some corner. In addition, the religious reflects the concern of Christ for the sick by his frequent visits, by offering to read appropriate passages of the Bible and to pray with the patient if this is desired. He provides the opportunity for the patient to encounter Christ in the sacraments, remembering that confession, Holy Communion and the Anointing of the Sick are usually great sources of strength and solace, especially when a person is terminally ill.

When the physician tells the truth about the illness, the patient is more open to accept this spiritual assistance and also has the opportunity to settle financial affairs, and resolve differences with family members and friends. He is given a sense of confidence and a feeling of control because he is allowed to make decisions regarding family and business matters. He feels included in future plans and thus will be in control of the situation to some extent. One patient, for example, expressed the hope that now he would begin doing all the things he wanted to do all his life, but felt he had no time to do.[6]

What about not telling the patient? First, there's a moral question. By the very fact of the relationship between doctor and patient, doesn't the patient have a right to this information? Second, in order to enlist the full cooperation of the patient in the treatment procedure, it seems he would have to know the reason for it. Third, even when patients are not directly informed, they usually find out their condition—either by themselves, or with the aid of other persons.

We live in an informed era. Patients are not stupid even though they are sick. They know that, generally speaking, radical surgery is not performed for a simple illness and that cobalt and chemotherapy are not given for a benign tumor. Besides, most patients, before surgery, experience fleeting fears that their illness is fatal and often think about cancer without anyone having introduced the subject. From previous surgeries on other family members and friends, they know the doctor reassures them immediately after surgery that no cancer was involved if that is the case.

One 32 year old mother of three young children had an inoperable malignancy in the abdomen. After the operation the surgeon told her he didn't know exactly what was wrong as he had not yet received a report on the biopsy he had sent away for analysis. Each day he came to check on her progress, she asked about the report, and he always said it hadn't come back yet. Finally, after five days, the surgeon informed her she had a tumor that required cobalt therapy. She replied she knew that already because he took so long to tell her anything.

Another 67 year old woman who had a terminal illness constantly asked about her condition but her four children refused to answer her truthfully and begged the doctor not to do so either. This woman, hospitalized for two months on this admission, gradually became weaker. Several times each day she made an inquiry about her illness and her children were always very quick to reassure her that everything would be all right. Because of her persistent questioning and because she was losing weight, the children placed a towel over the mirror in the room so that their mother could not look into the mirror and see how thin she was getting. This mother knew her condition in spite of all the children's efforts to hide it from her. She told the chaplain that this sickness must be much worse than the previous ones because the kids came in before visiting hours, stayed after visiting hours, and also visited more frequently than on previous admissions. Besides, she said she just felt much sicker than before.

Generally there are signs that communicate his condition to the terminally ill patient. First, no improvement lasts a long time; second, new symptoms are added to the old ones; third, the number and frequency of the visits of relatives increase; fourth, tension and worry are written on the faces of relatives and possibly the hospital personnel; and finally, sometimes the patient overhears snatches of conversations among family members or hospital personnel.

Another reason for informing the patient of his condition is that human relations are difficult enough without making them more complex by telling lies, especially when the patient will discover the truth sooner or later. Once the doctor and family have destroyed the patient's trust by lying to him, he will usually not believe them anymore, even when they are telling the truth.

The most devastating effect in deceiving the patient about his condition is that a communication barrier has been erected. By the deception the patient surmises that this subject is too horrible to discuss. The doctor and family have said in effect that he is forbidden to share his fears, anger, anxieties, and hopes with them because he isn't supposed to know his diagnosis. Now, the family has forced him to "play games" and act as if everything will be all right. It is tragic that loved ones who share so many intimacies in life abruptly stop communicating when it is most important for the patient to have someone with whom to share his deepest and troubled feelings.

The most painful aspect of dying is loneliness, and the greatest fears are isolation and abandonment.[7] The dying patient is crying out for companionship, for someone who is willing to listen when he wants to share his "gut" feelings about what is happening to him.

The minister of pastoral care assists the family by encouraging them to express their fears about informing the patient of his condition and pointing out to them the painful results of deceiving the dying person. In ministering to the patient the pastoral care person creates an atmosphere of openness, encouraging the patient to discuss any subjects and feelings he chooses. The minister works closely with the nursing personnel so that he knows how much information the patient has been given, what his physical condition is and how he is feeling each day before he visits him. In turn, the minister shares with the personnel any information he can so that they can assist the patient more effectively. In other words, they work together as a team for the welfare of the dying patient.

The family will often convince themselves that their loved one can't accept the truth about his terminal condition, that he will become depressed, that he will attempt suicide as a result of the knowledge of his terminal condition. What the family is really saying is that they can't accept this information, that it depresses them and they simply don't know how to cope with it. They don't want their loved one making them more anxious by bringing up the subject.

In addition, statistics indicate that incidents of suicide among terminally ill cancer patients who know they have cancer are only slightly higher than for the rest of the general population. The information about his cancerous condition does not depress a patient nearly as much as the fact that he has been deceived and treated as a child unable to handle the situation in a mature manner. The dying person also becomes depressed because he has no one with whom to talk about his feelings concerning his illness. He must keep all these feelings inside as he is not supposed to know how sick he really is and his family cuts him off whenever he says anything about his illness.[8]

Reaction of the Person to His Fatal Illness

During the last few years a number of studies have been made concerning the dying patient in an attempt to determine the emotions he experiences in the dying process. Dr. Elizabeth Kubler-Ross, who interviewed more than four hundred dying patients at Billings Hospital in Chicago concluded that patients usually go through five different stages in their attempts to cope with the fatal disease. The stages are: denial, anger, bargaining, depression and acceptance. She theorizes that if the patients are helped to work through these stages, they can reach the stage of acceptance which enables them to die with serenity and peace.

Using the study of Dr. Kubler-Ross as a basis for their investigation, the Career Development Corporation in 1971 produced a filmstrip explaining the stages of death.[9] This filmstrip makes a valuable contribution to the study of thanantology because the authors changed the name of the fourth stage to "grief" instead of depression, emphasizing the painful separation feelings the dying person experiences. These authors, then, emphasize separation rather than depression though admitting that both are present. They also indicate that not all patients go through all these stages and do not necessarily experience them in this order. It is too simplistic to say that all persons experience the same feelings in the dying process. People vary too much to say that every patient is angry, every patient is depressed. In addition, there are degrees of acceptance and for most patients there is neither complete acceptance nor total rejection of the fact that life is about to end.[10]

However, since the studies indicate that these emotions are experienced by many dying people, the pastoral minister is alert for their appearance so that he is ready to minister effectively when they occur. Special attention is given to denial because this is always mentioned in thanantology as a defense mechanism which the terminally ill employ. The information that the person will die and be annihilated is too painful to accept immediately and so he denies it. The fact that we human beings possess defense mechanisms like denial is another reason for informing the patient of his diagnosis. This gives him the opportunity of gradually allowing the information to come through or to continually reject it.[11]

The most common type of denial is the communication block, that is, simply to block the painful information out of a person's mind. A 55 year old man who had cancer of the lymph nodes in his neck illustrates this type of denial. After surgery, the physician informed him of his condition and told him he was scheduled to receive cobalt therapy to arrest the spread of the malignancy. Several minutes later, the chaplain visited this patient and when told that the doctor had just left the room, the chaplain asked if he had anything special to say. The man replied, "You know how doctors are. They're always in a hurry and never have time to tell you anything. I wanted to ask him a few questions, but didn't get a chance because he was gone before I knew it."

Another common form of denial people use is not to "give in" and to adopt an approach of carrying on business as usual. This type of person insists on continuing his routine schedule of employment long after common sense dictates at least a compromise allowing more time for rest and recreation. A middle-aged physician, for example, sustained an acute heart attack. His professional colleagues diagnosed his attack and advised immediate and absolute bed rest, quiet, and heavy sedation. The doctor patient stoutly refused to comply on the grounds of his heavy work schedule with his own patients. So he persisted in continuing his medical work and died suddenly in his office twenty hours later. This patient's personality was structured largely to deny any dependent emotional trends. He was a "self-made" man who labored hard to graduate from medical school, and continued working at a rapid pace to establish a practice, even to the extent of not permitting himself a vacation. In his personal life he lavished gifts on his family, but was Spartan regarding any self-indulgence.[12]

Ministering to the Dying Person

It is absolutely necessary for the pastoral care person in ministering to the dying patient to be sensitive to his own feelings. The sensitive minister knows his feelings about his own death and is comfortable with the thought that he too will die. He then uses his feelings as a barometer in understanding the patient and his family. What feelings are they experiencing? What stage of the dying process is the person presently in?

The religious is in touch not only with his own feelings about death, but also with his feelings about this dying patient's disease and the person himself. He asks himself how he feels about the particular disease and if he likes this person or not. If a minister is not in tune with his feelings, they become a weapon or a barrier preventing the dying person and his family from expressing their feelings or cause him to lack appreciation of the feelings that are being expressed. A minister's anxiety will only increase that of the patient who is very perceptive and easily picks up any uneasiness the people in the helping professions display.[13]

As a defense against this anxiety in speaking about death, one nurse suggested that a patient talk with the chaplain when he asked, "Nurse, does it hurt to die?" Just as her defense mechanism failed to meet his needs, so a clergyman fails in ministering to the dying person if he uses Sacred Scripture, prayer, and the sacraments as means of avoiding getting down to the "gut" feelings. A woman whose nephew died at the age of 21 after struggling against Hodgkin's disease for ten years described one such instance. "The chaplain assigned to the hospital," she sadly wrote, "stayed only long enough to administer the sacraments. My nephew wanted to talk to Father about death and the hereafter, but Father was always in such a hurry to leave. One day he asked the Methodist minister if he would say the stations with him. After the way of the cross, my nephew compared his sufferings with Christ's and found a great deal of peace of mind."

Not knowing the reaction of the religious person if the subject of dying is brought up, some patients will only hint at their desire to discuss death with leading statements like, "I wonder what's going to happen to the youngsters," or "I sure hope the kids make it through college." Other patients ask directly about their dying condition, such as the man who inquired, "Does it hurt to die?" In response to both situations, the pastoral care person urges the patient to explain what is behind the question by asking an open-ended question, one that doesn't allow for a "yes" or "no" answer. He might say, "How do you mean that?" or "I wonder what makes you ask that?" or "Let me sit down and you can tell me more about that."[14]

Part of being sensitive to the terminally ill person means that the minister is aware of the person's need from time to time to deny the finality of his sickness. Even after the dying person has admitted his condition, there are certain days when he uses denial because the thought of death and leaving his family is just too much for him to accept. On other days he admits his sickness and faces it realistically. The minister adjusts himself to the patient's mood and never imposes his need to discuss the subject of death on the patient. Rather, the pastoral care person walks with the dying person through the valley of the shadows of death. Sometimes the dying person sits down and rests for a while, and other times he moves through this valley. The minister adjusts to the needs and moods of the patient and waits to meet the patient's needs as they arise.[15]

From time to time the dying person and his family will become very angry at their helplessness in combating the disease. Sometimes God is blamed for the illness. When this happens, the patient and his family might begin blaspheming God or denying his existence, feeling that a good God would never allow this to happen. Immediately, the minster is tempted to defend God and offer other reasons for the sickness. God doesn't need anyone to defend him, and besides this approach only hinders the people from ventilating their angry feelings.

The pastoral minister encourages them to express their emotions and doesn't reprimand them for what is apparently disrespect to God. Rather he empathizes with them and reflects back their feelings. "It makes you angry that God allows this to happen. It doesn't seem fair." By doing this the people realize that someone understands what they are going through, and this fact in itself is very supportive.

Instead of expressing anger at God, the patient might express it at the person nearest to him. This could be a member of the nursing staff or the family. When this occurs to a relative, he or she is hurt, confused, and doesn't know how to act. Should the family member stay home for a few days and stop visiting? Should the relative apologize for some unknown wrong that was apparently committed?

Once a 23 year old man who was dying of terminal carcinoma in a hospital, voiced his anger at his widowed mother telling her that he didn't want her to come again. She was crushed by her son's anger and simply didn't know what to do. The next day, the son was sorry for his action and asked the chaplain to help him to seek his mother's forgiveness. Fortunately, the chaplain understood the young man's anger and called his mother and explained that her son was not really angry at her, but that his anger was one of the stages that people frequently go through in the dying process.

When a father dies, his daughter is being separated from one person, is losing a loved one. Yet losing this one loved father causes the daughter to experience grief, to be sad and to suffer pain because of her loss. The dying patient is separating, not just from one child, but from several people he loves dearly and from some objects he cherishes highly. Consequently, he suffers intensely and grieves.

Some dying patients are reminded every evening when they say goodnight to their families of the final goodbye at death, and as a consequence they find this daily goodbye very painful. To spare themselves this pain, some terminally ill patients begin separating from their families several days before their death by saying a final goodbye and requesting that only the spouse or one special person return to visit them. At this point such a patient is in grief, and the pastoral minister explains this to the family so they do not feel rejected but understand the stage of dying their relative is experiencing.[16] The minister also provides an opportunity for the patient to share his grief, to alleviate some of his intense feelings if he wishes to do so.

Even though the person is dying, he often clings to the last thread of hope of recovery and dreams of a miracle cure. It is cruel to destroy this hope, yet it is equally cruel to encourage it if it is totally unrealistic. So the pastoral care person supports the hope of recovery only to the extent that it is realistic. At the same time he allows the patient to express his hope of recovery in any way he choses. One woman, for example, expressed her hope by obtaining literature about several foreign countries in order to plan a vacation. This woman knew she wasn't going to leave the hospital, but enjoyed daydreaming about a European tour. A dying man expressed his hope by beginning to make plans "when the children are grown" and also spoke about "when this house gets too big for just the two of us."

The religious, aware that all dying persons are not entertaining the same kinds of hope, tries to determine each person's deepest hope. One patient hopes that everything is being done that is possible, another hopes he will never be abandoned, another that the pain will always be controllable, another that the Lord will constantly be his Good Shepherd and strengthen him. Finally, some patient hopes that his children will be taken care of or that his aged parent will not be neglected. Whatever it is that the patient hopes for, the pastoral care person is careful to acknowledge this and support it.

A final ministry to the dying person is to help him find some meaning in dying. Naturally, this differs for each individual and the pastoral minister cannot force his meaning on the patient. He searches with the person to discover some meaning in dying. The young man dying of Hodgkin's disease who was mentioned earlier was helped to find meaning by comparing his sufferings with those of Christ. Another person finds meaning by recalling that his sufferings in the dying process are an opportunity to gain help for a sinner to return to Christ. Another person makes sense out of his sufferings by concluding that he would rather die than be a burden to his spouse for many years. Still another person is helped by the sober thought that everyone has to die sometime or else the world simply would become too crowded, and that now is his time.

Ministering to the Family of the Dying Person

In ministering to the dying person, the religious gives a lot of attention and care to the family because they usually know the patient better than anyone else and love him deeply. Thus they are the best qualified to walk with the dying person through the valley of the shadow of death. In addition, their attitude toward the terminal illness and the patient affects his attitude and emotions for better or worse. However, in order for the relatives to be of great assistance, it is necessary that the lines of communication be open between them and the dying person. If the family cuts the patient off every time he brings up the subject of death, he loses the support of those closest to him. The minister indicates to the relatives that dying is made more bearable when the patient is allowed to express his fears because then his feelings of isolation and loneliness, the worst pain of dying, are alleviated.[17]

The religious assists the family in communicating with the doctor too. Often the treatments and procedures seem mysterious, haphazard, or even cruel to the uninstructed and emotion-laden family. At times, when the physician is explaining the illness and the treatment, the relatives are too upset to grasp what he is saying, and at other times they are using denial, refusing to accept the fact that their loved one is critically ill. The minister helps the family to understand the nature and goal of the medical program that the doctor has outlined. He repeats slowly the information already given to them when they have calmed down or lessened their use of denial. A surgeon, for example, informed a husband that his wife had a malignant tumor in her right breast and that a mastectomy operation was scheduled for the following day. The husband immediately concluded his wife had six months to live and became hysterical. The nurses called the chaplain and informed him of the circumstances. He sat down with the husband and asked him what the doctor had said. After repeating somewhat accurately the information he had been given, the chaplain asked if the surgeon mentioned anything about how long his wife would live after the operation. The husband shook his head, "no" and added, "but most people live only six months after cancer operations." The pastoral person then asked the distraught husband who told him that and he responded, "My friend died six months after his cancer operation." The chaplain explained that his experience at the hospital did not coincide with that and asked the nurse to give the man more medical information. When she finished her detailed explanation the husband was greatly relieved and was realistically hopeful about his wife's chances of survival. Further, a good samaritan reassures the family that everything possible is being done because this knowledge is comforting and helps to assuage some of the guilt the family often experiences at this time.[18]

Even though the medical facts have been clearly explained, the religious listens to learn how the family has understood them and what expectations they have as a result of this information. Gradually, they reveal certain expectations concerning the length of the illness, the pain involved, whether this will be the last hospitalization or not, and contemplate what life will be without their loved one. If the family goes through precipitate grief and is ready to give up their parent or spouse, and then he recovers enough to go home temporarily, the relatives could become very angry at the patient or the staff for putting them through all this worry again.

In ministering to the family, the pastoral care person is aware that no two families are alike even though they have some common denominators. Each family has its own rules, methods of communication and values, and he adjusts to each one. If he generalizes and acts as if all families react to the dying situation in the same manner, he misses many opportunities of ministering because he is not open to the unique manner each family has of coping with death. The pastoral person is also flexible because he needs to watch for the different stages the patient is likely to pass through in the dying process and keeps the relatives aware of the various stages the patient is passing through. Thus the ministry both to the patient and his family is dynamic and not static.[19]

Even though a dying person has not settled some personal property or financial investments, the relatives are hesitant to speak of these matters. They feel guilty about the advisability of settling these affairs because it seems so mercenary. The family should understand that these feelings are normal and they should not be ashamed of them. The religious encourages them to call in legal and financial advisors since other lives will continue on when the dying person's has ceased. Furthermore, the minister points out that the dying patient will probably be greatly relieved to know that he has taken care of these matters.[20]

Frequently, the family is confused about their own feelings concerning the approaching death of their loved one because of their own mixed feelings. One woman whose dying mother was 92 years old was torn apart with her ambivalent feelings. She wanted her mother to die so that she would not be suffering any more and yet she loved her dearly and dreaded the thought of living without her. It's helpful when a good samaritan urges the family to air their mixed feelings about the dying person, themselves, the hospital staff, and God. Relatives often become extremely angry because they can't change the course of the illness and as a result feel so helpless. They can also become very angry even at the dying person, if he was the decision-maker in the family, because now he seems to be abandoning them.

Because of faulty instruction in the churches it has been thought that it is wrong to express anger and so relatives are hesitant about voicing any negative emotions. The religious encourages the family to express their anger and assures them that it is not sinful because Christ himself was angry. After all, he threw the moneychangers out of the temple and knocked over their tables in anger. Our Lord constantly stressed that the message of Christianity is love, and the opposite of love is indifference, not anger. At least, if a person is angry he cares.

From what has been said, it is evident that the family experiences some of the same emotions that the dying person does. Realizing this, the religious ministers to the various needs of the relatives as they arise, just as he does with the dying person.

In order to minister effectively to the family, the pastoral person is sensitive to their focus of concern. The focus might be on themselves, on money or on reliving happy experiences of the past. Sometimes if the focus of concern is on recalling past happy experiences, the patient enjoys it because it takes his mind off his present illness. At other times the same focus causes the dying person to become angry because it makes him realize that he can no longer participate in the events.

Every family has an emotional history, and it is helpful for the minister to know as much as he can about it. When this family has encountered crises in the past, how did they cope with them? Did they escape from them, and thus have unresolved guilt, or did they walk calmly through them? How does this family deal with conflict among themselves? Do they usually cope with it by silence, by shouting at each other, by blaming one another, by withdrawing, or do they resolve the conflict by expressing their true feelings? Has this disease struck this family before and have they already watched a family member die from it? If they have, this could easily cause them to recall the previous death and stir up any unresolved guilt still present. If the disease is hereditary, guilt feelings could readily be increased among the relatives. It is also useful for the minister to know if the family keeps a sense of balance or if they are continually out of balance.

Ideally, at the same time that the minister assists the dying person in his search for some meaning in death, he helps the family to do the same thing. Again, he does not force his own meaning on them, but rather struggles with them in their attempt to discover their own meaning in the dying process so that they can achieve some satisfaction. If the relatives are engrossed in seeking pleasure, if their own happiness is their main goal in life, if all their efforts are spent on living in the proper section of town and on vacationing in just the right spot, then these people will have a difficult time finding any meaning in death and will need all the assistance the minister can provide.[21]

When the pastoral minister is "in tune" with his own feelings and the feelings of the dying person and his family, he becomes a catalyst helping all of them to work through their feelings about death. With his assistance, they can struggle together to deal with death, even though they may never reach the point of total acceptance.

NOTES

1. Elisabeth Kubler-Ross, M.D., *On Death and Dying* (New York: The Macmillan Company, 1969), p. 16.

2. Thomas P. Hackett, M.D., "Death as a Crisis," *Crisis Counseling for Physicians and Clergy*, Postgraduate Medical Education Seminar, University of Colorado, June 20, 1969.

3. Harvey Rothberg, M.D., "Patients and Physicians, Life and Death," *Pastoral Psychology*, February 1972.

4. C.M. Saunders, "The Management of Patients in the Terminal Stage," *Cancer*, edited by R.W. Raven (London: Butterworth, 1959).

5. Thomas P. Hackett, *op. cit.*

6. Schoenberg, Carr, Peretz, and Kutscher, "Management of the Dying Patient," *Loss and Grief* (New York: Columbia University Press, 1970), p. 240.

7. Carol Ren Kneisel, "Thoughtful Care for the Dying," *American Journal of Nursing*, March 1968, pp. 97-98.

8. Thomas P. Hackett, *op. cit.*

9. Career Development Corporation, "Care of the Terminally Ill," 1971, Glendale, California.

10. Harvey Rothberg, *art. cit.*

11. Paul H. Brauer, "Should the Patient Be Told the Truth." *Nursing Outlook*, Vol. 8, Dec. 1960, pp. 675-676.

12. Henry D. Lederer, M.D., "How the Sick View Their World," *Patients, Physicians and Illness*, ed. by Gartly Jaco (New York: Free Press of Glencoe, 1958), p. 253.

13. Rev. Carl A. Nighswonger, "The Terminally Ill Patient as Viewed by the Professional," *A Seminar on Terminal Illness* (Chicago: The University of Chicago Center for Continuing Education, April 18, 1970).

14. Rev. Edgar N. Jackson, "Pastoral Aspects of Death for Patient and Family," *Grief and Death Counseling*, sponsored by the Mental Health Association of Luzerne County, Kirby Health Center, Wilkes-Barre, Pa., October 1969.

15. *Idem.*

16. Robert Fulton, Ph.D., *Dying and Grieving*, Columbus, Ohio, April 29, 1971.

17. Thomas P. Hackett, *op. cit.*

18. Peter F. Regan, "Death and the Dying Patient," *Medical Insight*, Dec. 1969, p. 53.

19. Rev. Carl A. Nighswonger, *op. cit.*

20. Harold Fishbain, M.D., "Emotions of Intensive Care Patients and Their Families," Mercy Medical Center, Springfield, Ohio, Sept. 20, 1971.

21. Rev. Carl A. Nighswonger, *op. cit.*

SELECTED BIBLIOGRAPHY

Anonymous, "Death in the First Person," *American Journal Of Nursing*, Vol. 70, No. 2, February 1970.

"Aspects of Death and Dying," *Journal of the American Medical Woman's Association*, Vol. 19, No. 4, June 1964.

Beard, Bruce H., "Fear of Death and Fear of Life," *Archives of General Psychiatry*, Vol. 21, September 1969.

Bowers, Margaretta K., *Counseling the Dying* (New York: Thomas Nelson & Sons, 1964).

Conference on the Care of Patients with Fatal Illness, The New York Academy of Sciences, February 15-17, 1967.

Feifel, Herman, "Death," in Morman L. Farberow (ed.), *Taboo Topics* (New York: Atherton Press, 1963).

Foundation of Thanatology, *Bereavement and Illness* (New York: Health Sciences Pub. Corp., 1973).

Fulton, R.L., "Attitudes toward Death in Older Persons," A Symposium, *J. Geront.*, No. 16, 1961.

Fulton, Robert (ed.), *Death and Identity* (New York: John Wiley & Sons, Inc., 1966).

———, "Death and the Self," *Journal of Religion and Health* 3, No. 4, July 1964.

Glaser, Barney G. and Anselm L. Strauss, *Awareness of Dying* (Chicago: Aldine Publishing Co., 1968).

Hinton, J.M., *Dying* (Baltimore: Penguin Books, 1967).

Kneisl, Carol Ren, "Thoughtful Care for the Dying," *American Journal of Nursing*, March 1968.

Kutscher, A. and Michael Goldberg, *Caring for the Dying Patient and His Family* (New York: Health Sciences Pub. Corp., 1973).

Mayerson, Peter, "Death as a Crisis," Crisis Counseling for Physicians and Clergy, Postgraduate Medical Education Seminar, University of Colorado, June 20, 1969.

Mills, Liston O. (ed.), *Perceptives on Death* (Nashville: Abingdon Press, 1969).

Nagy, Maria H., *The Meaning of Death* (New York: McGraw-Hill Book Company, 1965).

Neale, Robert E., *The Art of Dying* (New York: Harper & Row, 1971).

Newmann, Eric, *Death Psychology and the New Ethic* (New York: Harper & Row, 1973).

Parsons, Talcott, "Death in American Society," *American Behavioral Scientist* 6, May 1963.

Rahner, Karl, *On the Theology of Death* (New York: Herder & Herder, 1964).

Riga, Peter J., "Death, Loneliness, and Love," *Cross and Crown*, December 1969.

Rome, Howard P., "Obligation to the Dying," *Medical Insight*, February 1970.

Rothenberg, Albert, M.D. "Psychological Problems in Terminal Cancer Management," *Cancer*, Vol. XIV, 1961.

Saunders, Cicely, "Terminal Patient Care," *Geriatrics*, Vol. 21, No. 12, December 1966.

Schnaper, Nathan, "Care of the Dying Person," *Psychiatry, the Clergy and Pastoral Counseling*, ed. by Dana L. Farnsworth and Francis J. Braceland, M.D. (Springfield, Ill.: C.C. Thomas, 1969).

Schoenberg, B. *et al.*, *Psychosocial Aspects of Terminal Care* (New York: Columbia University Press, 1972).

Shepherd, J. Barrie, "Ministering to the Dying Patient," *The Pulpit*, July-August 1966.

Tillich, Paul, *The Courage To Be* (New Haven: Yale University Press, 1952).

Verwoerdt, Adriaan, M.D., "Communication with the Fatally Ill," *A Cancer Journal for Clinicians* 15, 1965.

Verwoerdt, Adriaan, M.D. and Ruby Wilson, "Communication with Fatally Ill Patients," *American Journal of Nursing*, Vol. 67, No. 11, November 1967.

Weisman, Avery D., *On Dying and Denying: A Psychiatric Study Of Terminality* (New York: Behavioral Pub., 1972).

Wertenbaker, Lael Tucker, *Death of a Man* (New York: Random House, 1957).

Willis, Carol, "Letter," *Ladies' Home Journal*, LXXXVII, January 1960, Curtis Publishing Company.

Woodward, Kenneth L., "How America Lives with Death," *Newsweek*, April 6, 1970.

9. Ministering to a Family Immediately after Death

A group of funeral directors met with the Liturgy Commission of the Archdiocese of Cincinnati in the spring of 1972 to obtain a better understanding of the new funeral rite with its many options. At this meeting the undertakers suggested that the priest spend more time with the family immediately after a death, ministering to them and later helping them to select a suitable liturgy. They commented on the effective ministry of a number of Protestant clergymen who spend several hours following a death in the home of the bereaved helping them adjust to their loss. The minister is also often present when the family meets with the undertaker to discuss the many details of the funeral. Naturally, one detail discussed is the type of funeral service or liturgy that the family wishes to have. In contrast to this type of ministry, the Catholic priest usually only goes to the funeral home to conduct the wake service and at that time offers his condolences to the bereaved.

I feel that in many cases the priest fails to render this type of ministry not only because of his terrific work load, but mainly because he doesn't realize the need for his ministry, and because he feels uncomfortable as he doesn't know how to assist a family in grief. In this chapter I will offer several suggestions concerning the "dos" and don'ts" for any personal care person, priest, religious sister or seminarian, ministering to a family in grief.

Denial Followed by Expression of Emotions

Normally the first reaction a family has to the news that a

loved one has died is shock. This seems to be true even if the dying process has been long and the death is expected. The family frequently uses the defense mechanism of denial at this time because the information is too painful for them to accept immediately. They protect themselves against the pain by denying the facts that are explained to them. The clergyman doesn't try to take away the denial immediately because it might be beneficial for a particular family to use it briefly until they can cope with the sad news. Of course, if the denial continues for a period of time it becomes a serious problem and professional help is indicated.

The family can use several forms of denial but the most common is simply to block out the information, not to hear what is said. A mother, whose 6 year old son was killed in an automobile accident, illustrates three different ways of blocking out the painful information of his death in the following conversation with the coroner.

Coroner: Mrs. Jones, I'm the coroner and I have some bad news to give you. Your son was riding in the sports car tonight when it crashed. Unfortunately he was killed.

Mother: Oh, no. (Then she began to scream.)

Coroner: Mrs. Jones, I'm sorry to tell you your son is dead.

Mother: No, it can't be true. (Then she began to scream again and also to stamp her feet. After she regained her composure:)

Coroner: Mrs. Jones, I'm sorry. I know it's painful, but you must believe me. Your son is dead.

Mother: (The mother put her fingers in her ears) Can't you see, I'm not listening to you?

This mother used denial initially because the information was too painful to accept. It is interesting to note that each time she used a slightly different form of denial to block out the information. A father whose 20 year old son was killed in a similar accident denied his death initially in a slightly different manner saying, "You're wrong. You've made a mistake. You see I just talked with him an hour ago." In the movie *Summer of '42* the new widow anesthetized herself against the pain of loss by becoming drunk after she received a telegram informing her that her husband had been killed in action.

If a family uses denial to such an extent that it interferes with the funeral preparations, the clergyman ministers to them by reflecting on what is happening. He might say: "It doesn't seem possible your son could be dead because he seemed so healthy," or "It would be easy for you to deny your son is really dead." By doing this the clergyman gives them insight into what they are doing, and hopefully this will help them to face reality.

When the family has ceased using denial, they usually express emotion. Sometimes this is a flood of tears; other times it is screaming. A clergyman normally becomes very uncomfortable when this happens, and his impulse is to make an attempt to quiet them in some way. Nurses and doctors often become so upset at this point that they give the grievers sedatives. However, it's best to allow the bereaved to express their emotions in their own way, and not to impede their flow because hindering expression will only delay working through the grief.[1]

Many people who are suffering from the loss of a loved one feel guilty about an emotional expression of their grief because they think this is an indication of their lack of Christian faith in an afterlife. They misinterpret St. Paul's letter to the Thessalonians to mean, "Grieve not, as those who have no hope." St. Paul encourages an expression of grief though, because the correct interpretation of this thought is, "Grieve, not as those who have no hope."[2] I like to add to this, "But by all means grieve."

If the grievers keep their emotions bottled up, the emotional wound opens only partially when they are informed of the death of their loved one. A few days later the wound is widened when they realize more fully what has happened. It can be reopened several times before it becomes fully opened and healing begins to take place. On the other hand, if the bereaved express their feelings completely in the beginning, they develop a clean cut in their emotional wound, and then it can begin healing immediately.

During the expression of emotion the priest ministers to the family by being available and occasionally gently eliciting memories that carry great emotional impact. The more the bereaved talk about their feelings and the more they reminisce about the deceased, the more quickly they will be able to make contact with reality. In addition, they will loosen one by one the ties that bound them to the deceased.[3]

Some people in grief imitate the stoic manner of mourning that Jacqueline Kennedy showed as she was viewed on TV by millions across the nation during the funeral of her husband. Many commented on how strong she was, and others praised her for her self-control and composure. When a person loses a loved one, it hurts intensely just as it does when someone loses his leg or arm. The most natural thing in the world is to express this pain by crying and there's nothing shameful about it. This is true for men as well as women. Our society has an unwritten rule forbidding men to cry. Many times little boys are told after they fall hurting their knee: "Stop crying, you're a big boy now and big boys don't cry." However, men have emotions too, and it's helpful if they air them.

Emptiness of Pious Sayings

When the mourner has quieted down, the clergyman is tempted to say something because he feels people expect him to have some words of comfort that will soothe the painful feelings. In addition, the long silence becomes extremely uncomfortable and at this point attempts are often made to comfort the sorrowing with spiritual solace. However, these remarks are not heard because the bereaved is not listening, and furthermore the words are usually inappropriate, if not harmful.

Sometimes it's said: "I know what you're going through." How can anyone? No two people experience the same pain. When a mother of the family dies, each child suffers differently. For example, one son who is married has been very faithful to his mother and he feels a tremendous loss. Another married son has argued with his mother on many occasions, and so feels very guilty along with his grief. A married daughter is extremely angry with her deceased mother because she felt her mother tried to run her life by choosing her friends for her. So she feels anger and also grief. Another daughter who never married lived with her mother in a very dependent relationship and now she must live alone with no one to lean on. Thus she experiences feelings quite different from those of the other children.

Another spiritual consolation offered is: "It's God's will." This pious sermonette is extremely dangerous because it sometimes causes the family to hate that all-powerful God who took away their loved one. It could cause them to reject God entirely because they want nothing to do with a God who is supposed to be all good and yet permits tragedy.

When the sick person is elderly, suffering intensely, and there is no hope of recovery, the minister is tempted to say: "It's a blessing." This may be true, but it's best to allow the bereaved to express this thought because he may interpret the saying as being cold and insensitive when someone else says it. This platitude comes easily to a person outside the immediate family because his father or mother did not just die. However, the pastoral care person must not forget that no matter how old the parent is, or how long he has been incapacitated, it still hurts the sons and daughters when death comes.[4]

Other attempts to console the mourner that are ineffective are: "Time will heal," "It all happens for the best," "He's not suffering anymore," "He's in heaven now." All of these thoughts may be true, but immediately after the death of a loved one, they are meaningless, like water running off a duck's back. The mourners are suffering too much to hear what is said and besides at this time they are simply not prepared for this type of consolation.

It's important to remember that intense grief is 100% emotion. Thus, facts and logic do not make contact with the griever. One lady who wrote to Ann Landers after she experienced the death of her child said she wished that her friends and relatives would have skipped all the platitudes and simply have said:

"We care," "We love you," "I'm sorry." This mother felt that these simple sentences speak volumes and they do, because they are touching the mourner where he is, on the emotional level.[5]

Therefore the pastoral person ministers effectively by carefully selecting his words to comfort the bereaved, and generally the fewer the words the better. The presence of the clergyman in itself communicates concern and care for the family. He doesn't have to add much to what he is already saying non-verbally. He might from time to time reflect back the feelings the family is expressing, but spend most of his time ministering in silence.

Feelings of Guilt and Anger

After the bereaved has gone through the initial shock and emotionally expressed some of his grief, he usually begins to have feelings of guilt and anger. These emotions are directed toward oneself, the deceased, other people, and God.

A son may feel very guilty because he was not present at the moment his mother died, or because he put his mother in a nursing home, even though it was impossible to care for her at his home any longer. The clergyman's first impulse is to take away the guilt by assuring him he did all he could for his mother. It's much more helpful, though, to tolerate the irrational guilt and encourage him to talk about his guilty feelings in depth. After this, the pastoral person ministers effectively by helping him gain an insight into his feelings by asking a question which makes the mourner re-examine his feelings. For example, "You feel guilty because your mother died in a nursing home. Could you have given her nursing care 24 hours a day in your home?"

At other times the griever will express real guilt, remembering infidelities, losses of temper, thoughtlessness, etc. Again, it's best to urge the person to voice his feelings, and then the clergyman can calmly assure the griever of God's mercy and point out the many healthy, positive aspects of the love relationship. The clergyman is aware of the difference between real guilt and neurotic guilt and can help the person to obtain professional assistance, if neurotic guilt persists for some time.

Usually anger surfaces intermittently as the person works through his grief and sometimes it is directed toward the deceased. "Why did she walk out on me? Now that she's left me, what shall I do?" These feelings are quite normal and are experienced especially by dependent people, even when the deceased died from a cause beyond anyone's control i.e., incurable cancer. If the dependency is not too severe, the griever will probably work through these feelings, but unless new attachments equally gratifying are achieved, he may forever live in a state of relative adjustment with very little genuine acceptance.[6]

The mourner might also become angry at God, other people or fate. "Why should this happen to me?" and "What did I do to deserve this?" are expressions of anger against God or fate. In these circumstances the clergyman assists the griever if he allows the person to be angry at God, even to curse God for taking his loved one from him. This is difficult because the pastoral person feels compelled to jump in and defend God. But God doesn't need any defense, and besides, intellectual answers will not help at this point since the griever is on a very high emotional level. The same ministry of presence is effective if the griever becomes angry at the doctor, hospital, nurses, or the church. The person will gradually quiet down and in a few moments probably become apologetic for his actions.

The reaction of a son to his mother's death illustrates this point. The 22 year old son who had two married sisters was the youngest child in the family and the mother's favorite. Since he was not married, he lived at home with her even though he was making his own living. His mother, a 68 year old woman, had been operated on for a tumor in her kidney seven days before her death. At that time the surgeon told the family the tumor was malignant and had spread to other organs in the abdomen. The mother was recovering normally from the surgery when she suffered a cardiac arrest and died. As soon as the doctors tried to resuscitate her, the unit clerk called the family and all of them arrived before their mother was pronounced dead.

When all attempts to save the mother failed, a young intern came to an empty patient's room on the nursing unit where the chaplain and a nurse were trying to comfort the son and his two sisters. When the intern informed them that despite all their efforts their mother had died, the son immediately exploded. He began cursing vehemently and loudly in addition to pounding on the empty bed. He blamed the doctors for making his mother suffer unnecessarily by taking her to surgery and causing her to undergo the pains of post-surgical recovery. His sisters tried to quiet him urging him to watch his language in the presence of the chaplain, but this was to no avail. As soon as he began to air his feelings, the intern left. After several minutes, the son calmed down, and then the intern re-entered the room to ask the family if an autopsy could be performed. He hardly got the words out of his mouth, when the son with fire in his eyes shouted, "Hell, no. You've caused her enough unnecessary suffering already." The son continued to condemn the medical profession with vulgar expressions and gave way to his anger by pounding on the bed. Again his sisters tried to calm him but initially he paid no attention to them. After several more minutes, he sat down and became calm enough to help his sisters to select a funeral director and arrange for the burial. When the sisters got up to leave, the son turned to the chaplain and quietly asked to receive Holy Communion.

This young man had aired his feelings very openly and now was about to enter another stage of grief, beginning to accept the death of his mother. During the entire expression of these raw emotions, the chaplain said nothing, but was physically present for him and his sisters. He understood what the griever was experiencing and urged him to express his feelings, even though it took a somewhat violent form. No words were necessary, and besides the son would not have heard anything that was said.

Allowing Grief Work To Take Place

If the minister is assisting the griever at his home, he might be asked "to break the news" to the other relatives as they arrive. However, if the mourner can inform them himself, he should be encouraged to do so because explaining about the death to others will help him to work through his grief. The pastoral person is tempted to do everything for the griever. In this way, he feels he is contributing something and is not so uncomfortable just sitting there. Simply by being there he is doing something; his presence in itself communicates his concern and offers support to the griever.

A housemother for a midwestern university has had the task many times of informing college girls of the death of a parent. Usually the girl's friends want her to sit in a chair and do nothing while they make all the preparations for her to go home, i.e., they want to call the airport, pack her luggage, call a taxi, etc. This wise experienced housemother doesn't do any of these things. She is there with the grieving girl and assists her by her presence, and only makes preparations for her when she cannot do them herself. The housemother believes the distressed girl should do as much as possible for herself so that she can begin working through her grief. The effective clergyman will pattern his ministry after her example.[7]

When a child has died and his young brother has to be told of the death, the parents appreciate the clergyman's help. In an attempt to make it less painful for the brother to understand, some parents explain that God loves little boys so much that he took little Johnny to heaven to be with him. This sounds like a soothing approach, but it could easily cause the child to become extremely angry with the almighty God who stole his little brother and playmate from him.[8] The alert pastoral person warns the parents about the possible results of this approach and suggests a simple disclosure of the fact that the brother will not play with him anymore because he has died. After a short time, the sorrowing child should be told about heaven as a place of happiness after death.

In conclusion, the clergy chiefly ministers to a person in grief by allowing his presence to communicate his Christian concern and by remembering that his spirit communicates better than his words. Occasionally he reflects back what is taking place to indicate his acceptance of the griever and all his feelings and also to assist the griever in voicing his feelings. Finally, the pastoral care person strives to understand the griever, not necessarily to grieve with him, and by no means does he seek to have the griever understand him.

NOTES

1. Elisabeth Kubler-Ross, M.D., *On Death and Dying* (New York: The Macmillan Co., 1970), p. 6.
2. I Thessalonians Chapter 4, verse 13.
3. George C. Bonnell, "The Pastor's Role in Counseling the Bereaved" *Pastoral Psychology*, February, 1971, p. 29.
4. Rev. Carl A. Nighswonger, "Working with the Family of a Terminally-Ill Patient," *Seminar On Terminal Illness*, Chicago, Illinois, April 17, 1970.
5. Ann Landers, *Springfield Sun*, March 12, 1971.
6. George C. Bonnell, "The Pastor's Role in Counseling the Bereaved," *Pastoral Psychology*, February, 1971, p. 29.
7. Granger Westberg, *Good Grief* (Philadelphia: Fortress Press, 1961), pp. 15-16.
8. Elisabeth Kuber-Ross, M.D., *On Death and Dying* (New York: The Macmillan Co., 1970), p. 6.

SELECTED BIBLIOGRAPHY

Bachman, C. Charles, *Ministering to the Grief Sufferer* (Philadelphia: Fortress Press, 1967).
Beachy, W.N., "Assisting the Family in Time of Grief," *Journal of the American Medical Association* 202:559-560, November 6, 1967.
Becker, D. *et al.*, "How Surviving Parents Handled Their Young Children's Adaptation to the Crisis of Loss,"*American Journal Orthopsychiatry* 37:753-757, July 1967.
Belgum, David (ed.), *Religion and Medicine* (Ames, Iowa: Iowa State University Press, 1967).
Benda, Clemens, "Bereavement and Grief Work," *Journal of Pastoral Care* 16:1-13, Spring 1962.
Bruder, Ernst, E., *Ministering to Deeply Troubled People* (Philadelphia: Fortress Press, 1968).
Clinebell, Howard J., *Basic Types of Pastoral Counseling* (New York: Abingdon Press, 1966).
Elbert, Edmund J., *I Understand* (New York: Sheed and Ward, 1971).

Holst, Lawrence E. and Harold P. Kurtz (eds.), *Toward a Creative Chaplaincy* (Springfield, Ill.: Charles C. Thomas, 1973).

Jackson, Edgar N., *Understanding Grief* (New York: Abingdon Press, 1957).

Johnson, Paul E., *Psychology of Pastoral Care* (New York: Abingdon Press, 1953).

Kreis, Bernadine and Alice Pattie, *Up from Grief* (New York: The Seabury Press, 1969).

Kutscher, A., *Death and Bereavement* (Springfield, Ill.: Charles C. Thomas, 1969).

Lindemann, Eric, M.D., "Symptomatology and Management of Acute Grief," *The American Journal of Psychiatry*, September 1944.

Mitchell, Kenneth R., *Hospital Chaplain* (Philadelphia: Westminster, 1972).

Schoenberg, Carr, Peretz, and Kutscher, *Loss And Grief* (New York: Columbia University Press, 1970).

Wheelock, Robert D. (ed.), *The Updated Chaplain* (St. Louis: The Catholic Hospital Association, 1973).